ON EARTH AS IT IS IN HEAVEN

On earth as it is in heaven

THE KINGDOM OF GOD AND THE YEARNING OF CREATION

THE 2019 SWARTHMORE LECTURE

EDEN GRACE

First published October 2019

Quaker Books, Friends House, 173 Euston Road, London NW1 2BJ

www.quaker.org.uk

Enquiries should be addressed to the Publications Manager,
Quaker Books, Friends House, 173 Euston Road, London NW1 2BJ.

ISBN: 978 1 99931 413 2
eISBN: 978 1 99931 414 9

Book design by Cox Design, Witney

Printed by RAP Spiderweb, Oldham

Printed on FSC-certified paper from sustainably managed forests.

THE SWARTHMORE LECTURE

The Swarthmore lectureship was established by the Woodbrooke Extension Committee at a meeting held 9 December 1907. The minute of the committee provided for an "annual lecture on some subject relating to the message and work of the Society of Friends".

The name Swarthmore was chosen in memory of the home of Margaret Fell (later Fox), which was always open to the earnest seeker after Truth, and from which Quakers were sent loving words of sympathy as well as substantial material help.

The lecture is funded by Woodbrooke Quaker Study Centre and overseen and supported by the Swarthmore Lecture Committee, which is appointed by the trustees of Woodbrooke. It is a significant part of the education work undertaken at and from Woodbrooke.

The lectureship has a twofold purpose: to interpret to the members of the Society of Friends their message and mission; and to bring before the public the spirit, aims and fundamental principles of Friends. The lecturers alone are responsible for any opinions expressed.

The lectureship provides for the delivery of a lecture, usually at the time of Britain Yearly Meeting of the Society of Friends, and for its dissemination, usually in the form of a book. A lecture related to this publication was given by Eden Grace on Saturday 25 May 2019 at Yearly Meeting of the Religious Society of Friends (Quakers) in Britain, held at Friends House in London.

The Swarthmore Lecture Committee can be contacted at Woodbrooke Quaker Study Centre, 1046 Bristol Road, Selly Oak, Birmingham B29 6LJ.

www.woodbrooke.org.uk/swarthmorelecture

CONTENTS

ACKNOWLEDGEMENTS

The process of engaging with this topic and developing this lecture has been one of spiritual challenge and growth, of self-doubt and divine provision. In the 18 months since I first accepted the invitation to give this lecture, I have received unmerited grace and assistance from numerous sources, and I feel compelled to offer the deepest gratitude to:

- The Swarthmore Lecture Committee, for entrusting me with a task for which I felt wholly unworthy.
- The small committee appointed to accompany the development of this lecture: Simon Best, Maud Grainger, Oliver Robertson, and Martina Weitsch. I offer you a thousand apologies for the anxieties I caused in presenting you with a different kind of writing process than you anticipated. You have been steadfast in your support and encouragement of me, while also holding me accountable in ways that sometimes felt uncomfortable. You have been faithful, and I have grown under your oversight.
- Woodbrooke, for providing the nest out of which this message fledged and took flight, and Sandra Berry and Vik Grainger for making me feel so welcome.
- Earlham School of Religion, for providing office space during this project, thereby saving my family from a dining room full of photocopies, books and flipcharts.
- The General Board of Friends United Meeting, for recognising the spiritual peril of burnout and granting me a three-month sabbatical in which to renew my sense of call and connection to God. I am profoundly grateful especially to two general

secretaries – Colin Saxton and Kelly Kellum – who were able to prioritise the care of my soul over the productivity of my work. You have been the clearest examples of Christian leadership I have ever known.

- My colleagues at Friends United Meeting, for supporting and encouraging me in this project and for taking up my duties during my sabbatical, despite the fact that your plates were already full to overflowing.

- The Taizé Community, for bringing me into the presence of the Living Water that could replenish the aquifer of my soul at a critical moment.

- The Desert House of Prayer in Tucson, Arizona, for holding a sacred space of silence and contemplation within which words could arise from deep within and find their place on the page. Thanks especially to my fellow retreatant, Thich Phap Hai, and to Fr Tom, Sr Deb, Br Bill and Michael for companioning the stranger in your midst.

- Amy Gall Ritchie, for accompanying me in the work of faithfulness and for bearing witness to the exquisite beauty of life. When we meet, like the cousins Mary and Elizabeth, the Christ child in my soul leaps for joy.

- Wendy Parker, Lisa Parker, Larry Parker, Deanna Brooks, and Margie Parker, for encouraging me, for caring about me and the work I'm called to, and for telling me that you're proud of me.

- Isaiah Grace, Jesse Grace, Justin Campbell, and Achieng' Agutu, the children of my body and heart, for continually reminding me that I was made in the image and likeness of the Divine Parent.

- Jim Grace – what could I say that could possibly be adequate? You are my most steadfast companion and champion, never too exasperated with my foibles and always inspiring me to be my own best self. I am profoundly thankful to be doing life together with you, and to be joined with you in gratitude for the abundance of God's grace in our lives.

Additionally, the following individuals provided generous assistance with the content of this lecture. They shared freely of themselves in order to deepen my understanding. Any faults in the text are mine alone. Thank you to Margery Post Abbott, Timothy Ashworth, Nancy Bowen, Tracey Chantler, Ruth Cutcher, Ben Pink Dandelion, Eduardo Diaz, Jim Fussell, Isaiah Grace, Jim Grace, Gerard Guiton, Welling Hall, Michael Jay, Judy Lumb, Frederick Martin, Hezron Masitsa, Suzanna Mattingly, Kevin Mortimer, Walid Mosarsaa, Farhat Muhawi, Lama Murra, Kees Nieuwerth, Jay O'Hara, Marjorie Parker, Diane Randall, Janet Scott, Christian Sharits, Heather Strathearn, Joel Tishken, Robert Wafula, and Rodgers Wekesi.

A *note about inclusive language*

I have endeavoured to use inclusive language at all times whenever referring to humanity, and I have tried as much as possible to construct sentences that do not require a pronoun in reference to God. The latter has not always been possible, and there are some names of God that are inherently gendered, such as Father (and also Mother Hen, one of my favourite names of God, from Matthew 23:37 and Luke 13:34). I have not edited the language used by others when I have taken a direct quotation from a published source, so gendered language persists in those passages. I take it as a given that God is not actually a gendered being, and that our human languages and relational metaphors will always fall short of a full and accurate understanding of God's own nature and relationship with the beloved creation. I invite you to enter into the poetry of biblical language and receive the specific wisdom that each name and metaphor might have to offer.

CHAPTER I

The Kingdom is come and coming: 'realising' eschatology as the source of Quaker concern for creation

Introduction

The first song from the Taizé Community in France that I ever learned was 'Jesus, Remember Me when You Come into Your Kingdom'.[1] It is one of the most widely beloved of their songs, voicing as it does the words of the thief who hung on the cross next to Jesus, deeply aware of his own unworthiness and yet appealing to Jesus for mercy.[2] It captures the hope we can sometimes grab hold of, even in the most hopeless situation – the assurance that there is a future awaiting us in which we will be cherished, remembered, forgiven, and allowed to flourish. This dark night on the cross will not last forever; morning will come.

This hope – this assurance of a coming *rightness* that will rectify all that is wrong with the present – is fundamental to Christian faith. We know that this present reality is not as it should be. It is not as God wills it to be. We know that in this present world, evil sometimes does prevail for a season. We despair at how far off the mark of God's *shalom* our families, communities and nations have fallen. And yet, this despair does not have the last word. For there is a Light that shines in the darkness, and the darkness has not, will not, can not, *not ever*, put it out.[3]

The subdiscipline of theology that explores this promise of hope is called 'eschatology',[4] and it is a wild and woolly place. Here you find the sublime and the bizarre, the speculative and the psychotic. There are horsemen and angels; thrones and fiery pits; cities descending from the clouds and people being snatched away in an instant; unprecedented environmental catastrophes and a glorious

---

1 The recording I played at the beginning of the spoken lecture of this book can be found at www.youtube.com/watch?v=o4LPVWWwhfs.
2 Luke 23:42.
3 John 1:5.
4 In this chapter in particular – but also in the overall concept of this lecture – I am deeply indebted to the book *Heaven on earth: Quakers and the Second Coming* by Ben Pink Dandelion, Douglas Gwyn and Timothy Peat. I first read this book in 1999 as part of my seminary studies, and I'm thrilled that it has recently come back into print. Its thesis – that the central experience of early Friends was "the present sense of the Second Coming of Christ and the bringing of heaven on earth" (back cover) – has remained the foundation by which I have understood all of Quaker theology, ethics, ecclesiology, soteriology, missiology, and spirituality. While I have been deeply shaped and formed by this extraordinary book, the authors bear no responsibility for whatever weaknesses appear in my own theological writings.

new creation; weapons turned into farm implements; lions lying down with lambs; and children leading the people of God. The study of eschatology, by definition, raises profound and perilous epistemological[5] questions: how do we know what we think we know about what is yet to come? On what basis do we gather and evaluate this data? How do we discern divine revelation from human delusion?

We are right to engage in a conversation about eschatology with trepidation, yet engage in it we must, because without doing so it is impossible to discover our authentic response to climate change.

The Kingdom in the teachings of Jesus

What is the 'Kingdom of God'? What did that term signify for Jesus? There is one point I should make right away: the Kingdom of God is *not* the same thing as the apocalypse described in Revelation, nor is it synonymous with the end times, nor with the Second Coming of Christ, nor with heaven, nor the afterlife. Nor are any of these concepts synonymous with each other! The popular sci-fi-mytho-religiosity of our time has so confused this matter that it takes conscious effort on our part to detangle these associations in our mind – to hear Jesus and the early Friends for what they are actually saying.

In order to do this, we have to recognise that the Kingdom of God forms a central pillar of Jesus's ministry. It was one of his most frequent topics of teaching, almost always by way of parable. Gerard Guiton claims that "the Kingdom was the very *raison d'être* for Jesus' mission, his life and death, and his testimony to restored unity with God" (Guiton, 2009: 30). What is this Kingdom? What was Jesus trying to convey to his followers in all of these stories? What does it tell us about the hope we have, here and now?

The Greek word *basileia* appears 163 times in the New Testament, and it is nearly always translated as 'Kingdom'. The majority (113) of these instances occur in the three synoptic gospels (Matthew, Mark and Luke), and almost all of these are contained within the spoken words of Jesus. In Matthew, the Greek phrase is "the Kingdom of Heaven". In all the other books of the New Testament, it is "the

---

5 Epistemology is the philosophical study of the nature, sources and criteria of knowledge. It asks the question, 'How do we know what we know?'

Kingdom of God". (For our purposes we can consider these to be equivalent terms.) Without a doubt, this Kingdom theme was of primary importance for Jesus.

So, what is signified by this word *basileia*? First of all, in Greek it does not convey the specific sense of territory, as it does in English. It does not refer to a certain piece of land or a location on a map, but rather to the work and authority of a king. A *basileia* is all that which is under the sovereignty, power and control of a king. A deep study of the Greek by a scholarly translator led to the uncovering of nine different nuances of meaning of *basileia*, which could be collapsed into two primary meanings: God establishes God's rule, and God renews the world (Kassühlke, 1974). To enter into the Kingdom of God is to put oneself under the authority of God the king, in a renewed world. When Friends say they are living in the Kingdom, they mean that they are living under the direct authority of God and in holy obedience to God's will, in accordance with Jesus's teachings, as God transforms all creation anew.

It is perhaps most useful to think of *basileia*, the Kingdom of God, as a symbol.[6] Unlike a concept, a symbol cannot be exhaustively defined. It lives more in the connotative realm of poetry than in the denotative realm of discursive speech. Although the use of the word 'Kingdom' to refer to God's activity inevitably recalls all prior associations with human kingdoms, the grammar of its usage makes it impossible for it to rest in those associations. "That it is 'preached', 'announced', and 'revealed', and that it 'comes', indicate that its structural network is discongruent with kingship, since these are not terms identified with kings" (Scott, 1989: 58). A symbol like this does not have a one-to-one referent but has instead, to use Umberto Eco's terminology, a "content nebula" (Eco, 1984: 144). What are some of the elements of that nebula?

In the ears of Jesus's followers, his teachings about the Kingdom would have immediately brought to mind the prophecy of Daniel as he interpreted the dream of King Nebuchadnezzar:

6   In this section I am indebted to Scott (1989) and his discussion of the Kingdom of God as a "tensive symbol" (56–62), in which he draws upon Perrin (1974) and Eco (1984). Would that I could divert from the main path of this lecture and delve into the delicious feast of semiotics (the study of symbols and their interpretation) in biblical hermeneutics! Alas, let me instead recommend these sources to the interested reader.

> And in the days of those kings [read: global empires] the God of heaven will set up a Kingdom that shall never be destroyed, nor shall this Kingdom be left to another people. It shall crush all these kingdoms and bring them to an end, and it shall stand forever.[7]

The 1st-century Hebrew people, living under brutal occupation by the Roman Empire, clung fervently to this particular prophecy as a promise that one day the oppressive imperial powers of this earth and their cruel kings would be overturned, and all creation could live freely and in peace under divine leadership. Thus, the Kingdom of which Jesus spoke captured the imagination and sparked the hope of the people precisely because it stood in opposition to the kingdoms of this world.

Biblical scholar Bernard Scott (1989) identifies the Kingdom parables of Jesus as diaphoric metaphors – metaphors that jolt the hearer with surprising or paradoxical associations. Most of us have heard these parables all our lives, and so they have become commonplace to us, but consider afresh how bizarre it is that Jesus would compare God's activity to that of a woman sweeping her house[8] or making bread,[9] or that he would compare the Kingdom to a lavish royal banquet for the homeless and unwashed.[10] These shocking and subversive stories overturn everything we thought we knew about the behaviour of 'the king' and implicitly judge the kingdoms of this world by contrast.

The phrase "your Kingdom come, your will be done, on earth as it is in heaven", from Matthew's version of the Lord's Prayer, emphasises this theme of contrast and reversal between the two types of kingdom, two forms of leadership, two sources of authority or will – what we currently see on earth and what we hope for in God. It is what makes the symbol of the Kingdom of God so potent and subversive.

Many people today are rightly uncomfortable with the masculine imperial model of God implied by the term "Kingdom of God" and

---

7   Daniel 2:44 NRSV.
8   Luke 15:8–10.
9   Matthew 13:33.
10 Luke 14:16–24.

wish to substitute a more egalitarian term. I'm aware that this lecture is being given to a group of people who have the word 'Kingdom' in the name of their country, and I appreciate that this may colour their response to the term, positively or negatively. For me, working as I have done for the past 15 years in post-colonial contexts, the profound evils of empire are indisputable. The generational trauma of colonialism is, in my mind, the single most important sociological factor in undertaking ministry in these contexts today.

It is precisely because of this conviction that, unlike some others,[11] I am unable to substitute a gentler word. I'm not ready to surrender the concept that God-as-King stands in opposition to all human kings and kingdoms, and subverts all we think we know about power. The revolutionary impact of the term 'Kingdom of God' rests as much on what it stands *against* as on what it stands *for*, and as much on what kind of power it *refutes* as on what kind of power it *represents*. The many attempts at finding more congenial synonyms have not succeeded in retaining this edgy contrast.

The Kingdom of God in the spiritual experience of early Friends

So, having understood something about the scriptural content nebula of the Kingdom of God, let us turn to an examination of how this symbol functioned for early Friends.

But first, a note about early Friends' writings: with a few exceptions, early Friends were not particularly concerned with writing systematically. They were deeply concerned with conveying the truth through phenomenological language. They wrote experientially, not dogmatically, and were very clear about the fact that their words were inadequate as means of conveying their experience.[12] In their writings they drew upon biblical allusions that would have resonated deeply within their context but that can often be lost on us biblically illiterate Friends today, resulting, for us, in a shrinkage of the content nebula. In their unsystematic way, they

---

11 Most notably Guiton in a 2019 essay published online under the title *Where heaven and earth are one: Following 'the way', caring for the planet.*

12 For example, George Fox said about his experiences of 1647: "And I saw into that which was without end, and things which cannot be uttered, and of the greatness and infiniteness of the love of God, which cannot be expressed by words" (Fox, 1952: 21).

were entirely comfortable with a mode of expression that we today would call 'theopoetic',[13] using what Carole Spencer described as "a distinct biblical–mystical–symbolical language" (Spencer, 2004: 134). They used words to express that which words cannot reach. They played with grammar and sentence structure, such as in the evocative verb tenses in the phrase "the day of the Lord is come and coming", which appears in the works of several early Friends (e.g. Edward Burrough and James Parke). They resisted the demand of their critics that they make precise definitions and categorical doctrines out of their spiritual experiences. They found their experience to be well reflected in biblical language, and they gave full flowering to the expressive use of that language.[14]

Gerard Guiton claims, and I would agree with him, that "the principal goal of the early Friends was to preach the Kingdom and to live it" (Guiton, 2009: 38). It was one of their most fertile spiritual symbols. They saw the structures and practices of the established institutional church as prideful artefacts of the apostasy[15] and felt compelled to call people to an "inward endtime covenant which eschews the need for outward rite and form" (Dandelion and Martin, 2015: 119). They were accused of overly spiritualising the historical work of Jesus (and this might indeed be a fair criticism of us today), but in fact their message was much more integrative and more revolutionary than that:

> Quakers were simply connecting [the] cosmic outward activity of Christ with the spiritual rebirth within believers. … If this collapses the eternal into the personal, as the critics averred, it also telescopes the personal back out into the eternal, providing individuals with a thrilling sense of participation in history and communion with the divine, grafting them into the body of God. (Dandelion and Martin, 2015: 130)

---

13 To learn more about theopoetics, I recommend www.artsreligionculture.org.

14 For a deeper discussion of the language of early Friends' spiritual experience, see Brian Drayton and William Taber's *A language for the inward landscape* (2016).

15 Apostasy is defined as a falling away or abandoning of the true faith. Early Quakers, like other radical Christians of their time, believed that the early church ceased to be the church of Jesus Christ when it became the official state religion of the Roman Empire in the 4th century, and that state churches had continued in this condition of apostasy until their present time.

To live in the Kingdom is to be united with the power and love of God, and to participate in God's work of transformation in the world, right here, right now.

Theosis: participation in the Kingdom

I have been interested in the Eastern Orthodox branch of the Christian church since the beginning of my involvement with the World Council of Churches, and I spent time studying Orthodox theology in order to understand the tradition better. One of the things I found (and this insight is by no means original to me) was that there are some very strong similarities between Quakers and Orthodoxy. It might even be said that Quakers have more in common with the Orthodox churches than we do with either Protestants or Catholics.[16]

One of the most compelling similarities, to me, is with the Orthodox doctrine of *theosis*, also called deification. It is a hard idea to explain and easily misconstrued. The traditional simple formulation is that "God became man so that man can become God".[17] But, of course, this is both confusing and somewhat alarming. A better way to say it would be that God united God's self with humanity so that humanity could be reunited with God.[18] This is the entire purpose of human life.

This concept of participatory union – of the spiritual experience of being united with God and participating in God's love – is very consistent with Quaker spiritual experience. For me, at least, this is a much more satisfactory description of 'salvation' than anything Protestant theology offers.

---

16 Certainly, our understanding of the nature and form of worship is closer to the Orthodox tradition of *hesychasm* (mystical experience of the Light of the Transfiguration (Tabor Light) through silent contemplation (*theoria*)) than it is to either the Roman Catholic/Anglican liturgy or the Protestant service of remembrance.

17 This formulation is normally attributed to St Athanasius of Alexandria, a 4th-century Egyptian theologian.

18 Within the Orthodox theological tradition, great emphasis is placed on the triune nature of God – that God, in God's very essence, is a loving relationship between three distinct persons. Priority is placed on the relationality (*perichoresis*, or mutual envelopment) of the Trinity, rather than on God's static attributes. Within this intimate concept of God as love, it becomes possible to envision humanity participating in that love, as the child participates in the love between the parents.

Whereas the Orthodox Church places great significance in the outward sacraments, especially the Eucharist, we Friends consider the true communion to be an inward spiritual experience rather than an outward human ritual. Especially in meeting for worship, but also in every moment of a life lived in holy obedience, we can experience a true communion with the body and blood of Jesus, not through physical symbols but through incarnational living. Through the inbreaking of the Kingdom.

Marks of the Kingdom

In the preaching and lived experience of early Friends, we can discern certain themes which serve as eschatological signs – marks that we are truly participating in the Kingdom that is come and coming.

Time

For early Friends, the Kingdom transcended our linear experience of time, but it was not a spiritualised or otherworldly reality. Participation in the Kingdom brought with it an acute sense of the eternal within the present, always in the process of inbreaking into human hearts, communities and history. It had much less to do with a roadmap of things to come, and much more to do with the nature of things as they truly are in the present moment. George Fox wrote this piece of advice in a 1652 letter to his parents: "Look not back, nor be too forward, further than ye have attained; for ye have no time, but this present time: therefore prize your time for your souls' sake" (Fox, 1831: 19).

In England during the 1630s–1660s, insurgent premillennial[19] groups were proclaiming the imminent Second Coming of Christ (with violent political consequences). In this milieu, "Friends distinguished themselves from these speculators of the apocalypse

---

19 Premillennialism is the belief that the Second Coming of Christ will occur *before* the thousand-year reign of Jesus on earth, and that his coming will be accompanied by a cataclysmic tribulation. *Post*millennialism expects Jesus to come again *after* a thousand-year period of peace and justice on earth. Obviously, there are profound ethical implications in these alternatives. Premillennialists anticipate that things will get worse and worse until Jesus comes. Postmillennialists expect things to get better and better until Jesus comes. (A third option, *a*millennialism, is propounded by most liturgical churches; it claims that the symbolic language of a thousand-year reign is meant to signify the era of the church.)

by finding the anticipated future arriving in their present, as they described their experience of new spiritual birth in the midst of social turmoil as the Second Coming of Christ within themselves and their communities" (Martin, 2012: 3). Friends therefore had a different approach to the whole question of time and sequence. They believed themselves to be experiencing God's time (*kairos*), which was of an entirely different character from linear clock time (*chronos*). In Bill Taber's beautiful words: "The *was* can become the *is*, or the *to be* can become the *is now*" (Taber, 1980: 12). And, as Doug Gwyn puts it:

> The strength of early Quaker eschatology was to keep all questions about the future grounded rigorously in the present, just as it kept all questions of theology and politics grounded tenaciously in practical terms. Eschatologies that emphasize present realization are sometimes classified as 'realized eschatologies'. 'Realizing' is probably a more apt description in the early Quaker case, since Friends viewed present realization as part of a larger, unfolding reality, neither totally present nor totally future. (Gwyn, 2018: 109)

This dialectic between the 'already' and the 'not yet', and the mystical union between the two as we participate in the unfolding of the present moment, shows up clearly in two extracts from Edward Burrough, a prolific writer who died in 1662 while imprisoned for his faith (see Dandelion and Martin, 2015). In these passages, Burrough is writing to encourage Friends to be steadfast in the face of persecution. In the first, he emphasises the 'already', the 'is come':

> The new Jerusalem is come down from Heaven, … and unto you an entrance is given, and the way is prepared, and the marriage of the Lamb is come. (Burrough, 1672: 65)

And, in this second extract, the 'not yet' or 'is coming' is in focus:

> How long Lord? How long? When wilt thou appear to lay their [the persecutors'] honour in the dust of confusion? … How

long shall the Remnant of Sion sit as a Widow, bemoaning her Children? ... Come Lord Jesus, come quickly. (Burrough, 1672: 114)

In other words, in this present suffering, we are already participating in the new Jerusalem, the Kingdom of God, which is truly come. And yet we still await the day of the Lord, when Christ will come to judge the earth, including those who persecute us. Past, present and future are collapsed into the mystical union of this present moment, and the experience of this present moment is telescoped into eternal significance.

Unity

As Fox preached his message among the dissatisfied, dispirited and disorganised Seekers of the North, great crowds were converted, and one of the immediate fruits of this conversion was an experience of unity among themselves. In his beautiful description of the effects of the great Firbank Fell sermon, Francis Howgill says:

The Kingdom of Heaven did gather and catch us all, as in a net, and his heavenly power at one time drew many hundreds to land,[20] that we came to know a place to stand in and what to wait in; and the Lord appeared daily to us, to our astonishment, amazement, and great admiration; insomuch that we often said unto one another with great joy of heart, "What, is the Kingdom of God come to be with men?" ... From that day forward our hearts were knit unto the Lord, and one unto another in true and fervent love, not by any external Covenant, or external Form; but we entered into the Covenant of Life with God; and that was a strong obligation or bond upon all our spirits, which united us one unto another. ... And thus the Lord, in short, did form us to be a people for his praise in our generation. (Howgill, 1672)

---

20 Referencing John 21:6.

The people, who had not until that point known themselves to be a people, were now intensely bonded to each other through a shared spiritual experience (rather than a shared confession or creed). The mark of unity as an eschatological sign persists to the present day among Friends, in our practice of making decisions as a community. While in traditional Christian theology, the mark of unity is understood to signify the common baptism of the community under the bishop in apostolic succession, and thus to the unbroken historical experience of the Christian community, for Quakers the mark of unity is understood as a sign of the direct and unmediated revelation of the will of God through the inbreaking of God into our communal life.

Transformation of the world
Early Friends often cited Jesus's teaching in Luke 17:

> Once Jesus was asked by the Pharisees when the Kingdom of God was coming, and he answered, "The Kingdom of God is not coming with things that can be observed; nor will they say, 'Look, here it is!' or 'There it is!' For, in fact, the Kingdom of God is among [or within] you."[21]

This resonates deeply with our Quaker spiritual practice of the continual obedience to the inward light of Christ. There is, however, a danger here that many liberal Friends have fallen into, of equating the Kingdom of God solely with personal spiritual experience. Such a privatised Kingdom belies Jesus's intentions and neglects the cosmic significance of the *basileia*. In such a time as this, when we are facing real cosmic peril, a privatised Kingdom will not do.

For early Friends, their experience that the Kingdom is come and coming had real-world social and political consequences, and demanded real risk-taking from them. They were led into such provocative acts of civil disobedience and disruption that they were routinely whipped, imprisoned and deprived of their property. These courageous acts did not emerge from the careful strategising of a committee. Rather, they were the almost-inevitable consequences

---

21 Luke 17:20–21 NRSV.

of the transformation wrought by the Kingdom as it overpowered their lives, leading them to an entirely counter-cultural embodiment of power, which they named the Lamb's War.[22]

Early Friends exemplified the spiritual ethos of the Book of James: a synthesis of faith and action not as two things that must be held in balance in the Christian life but as one seamless thing. "For just as the body without the spirit is dead, so faith without works is also dead."[23] To be a citizen of the Kingdom of God was to be led into revolutionary faithfulness, a theme explored in the section below on testimony. There was nothing 'private' about it.

Perfection

An important eschatological theme of early Friends was the restoration of humanity to a condition before the Fall, often referred to as 'perfection' (see especially Connell, 2014; Hinshaw, 1964). This holiness experience was an authentic thread in Quakerism from the very beginning, however much it might have become decontextualised by the influence of the Wesleyan Holiness movement in a later century.[24] Whatever we might think about the plausibility of George Fox's claim, it was central to Fox's spiritual experience and teachings that he knew himself to be in a condition even superior to that of Adam before the Fall, because he felt himself to be beyond even the susceptibility to sin.

---

22 From Revelation 17, about the role of Jesus in overturning the empires of this world. The reference to Jesus as the Lamb in the Revelation text evokes the declaration of John the Baptist in John 1 that Jesus is "the Lamb of God who takes away the sin of the world". In this way, Jesus is understood as the ultimate Passover lamb (referring to Exodus 12), whose sacrifice on the cross removes any need for continued ritual sacrifice in the temple.

23 James 2:26 NRSV. It is interesting to note that this central affirmation of James directly contradicts the separability thesis of Descartes that forms the basis of all western intellectual dualism, as discussed in the section on Genesis 1 (chapter 3, footnote 11).

24 In the second half of the 19th century, Friends were influenced by two somewhat opposing trends in religious thought: modernism and evangelicalism. During this time, Friends of the more evangelical persuasion found great resonance between the Wesleyan doctrine of Holiness and the Quaker doctrine of Perfection. Certainly, the points of connection between the two are real and important, especially as they both prioritise participation in, and union with, Christ. However, Spencer (2004) claims that the embrace of Wesleyanism represented a rediscovery of essential Quakerism. I am not convinced by this claim because it seems to neglect the centrality of realising eschatology in Quaker soteriology, a point that would distinguish it from Wesleyan soteriology. Without the eschatological aspect, Wesleyanism constructs a two-stage salvation (justification and sanctification) that seems quite alien to Quaker experience.

He knew that he did not achieve this condition by ethical striving but by the grace of God, through the "flaming sword",[25] his preferred metaphor for the divine power over sin. Permit me to quote from an entry in Fox's journal dated 1648–1649 at some length:

> Now I was come up in spirit through the flaming sword, into the paradise of God. All things were new; and all the creation gave unto me another smell than before, beyond what words can utter. I knew nothing but pureness, and innocency, and righteousness; being renewed into the image of God by Christ Jesus, to the state of Adam, which he was in before he fell. The creation was opened to me; and it was showed me how all things had their names given them according to their nature and virtue. … But I was immediately taken up in spirit to see into another or more steadfast state than Adam's innocency, even into a state in Christ Jesus that should never fall. And the Lord showed me that such as were faithful to Him, in the power and light of Christ, should come up into that state in which Adam was before he fell; in which the admirable works of the creation, and the virtues thereof, may be known, through the openings of that divine Word of wisdom and power by which they were made. (Fox, 1952: 27)

For this claim, Friend George was convicted of blasphemy and imprisoned. One can certainly see how the claim to be superior to Adam would have caused offence! But, to Fox, the contrary claim was even more offensive. If it is not possible for humans to be truly liberated from sin, then what efficacy had the cross? In 1674 he said that "they that denied perfection[,] denied the work of the ministry, and the gifts which Christ gave" (Fox, 1952: 688). To him, it must be the case that God is capable of achieving that which God intends to do, otherwise God would not be God.[26]

---

25 The sword that guarded the entrance to the Garden of Eden after the banishment of Adam and Eve in Genesis 3:24.

26 It was left to Robert Barclay to make systematic sense of the doctrine of perfection, which he expertly did in the Eighth Proposition. The Barclay version is considerably less scandalous than what Fox claimed about his own experience.

We don't 'earn' perfection through moral striving, for (as both Paul[27] and Martin Luther[28] were acutely aware) we will always fall short in our striving and double back into even deeper despair. Fox's early life reflects this same moral anguish in the inability to perfect oneself. What he discovered through direct spiritual experience, not through the teachings of any religious leader, was that he could receive purification and perfection as a free gift of God. And he learned and taught that, in order to be maintained in that state, we are to be continually faithful to the risen and present Christ, who is even now guiding us in a daily living of holy obedience that we call testimony.[29]

We may pause here to notice some important ecological themes in the Fox passage above, especially as they relate to the eschatological experience of perfection. Note that as Fox passed through the flaming sword (the entryway into the Garden of Eden) and ended the exile from paradise, he didn't find himself in the old garden but in a place that was brand new (presumably the new Jerusalem of Revelation 21). In that place, which was certainly a place of physicality, not simply ethereal, he found that he had heightened senses and could perceive truths about the created world beyond what was possible before. His experience echoed that of Isaiah, who heard God exclaim, "I am about to do a new thing; now it springs forth, do you not perceive it?"[30] Like Adam in Genesis 2:19, Fox was given a multi-sensory perception of the

---

27 "I do not understand my own actions. For I do not do what I want, but I do the very thing I hate. ... I can will what is right, but I cannot do it. For I do not do the good I want, but the evil I do not want is what I do" (Romans 7:15, 18b–19 NRSV).

28 "When I was a monk, I made a great effort to live according to the requirements of the monastic rule. I made a practice of confessing and reciting all my sins, but always with prior contrition; I went to confession frequently, and I performed the assigned penances faithfully. Nevertheless, my conscience could never achieve certainty but was always in doubt and said: 'You have not done this correctly. You were not contrite enough. You omitted this in your confession.' Therefore, the longer I tried to heal my uncertain, weak, and troubled conscience with human traditions, the more uncertain, weak, and troubled I continually made it. In this way, by observing human traditions, I transgressed them even more; and by following the righteousness of the monastic order, I was never able to reach it" (Luther, 1955: vol. 27, 13).

29 Connell (2014) is very helpful in showing that Quakers managed to forge a 'middle way' between Augustine (and later Calvin) and Pelagius. The crux of the argument between these two was whether humans have the ability within ourselves to choose good (it being a given that, after the Fall, humans have the ability to choose evil). This is essentially the question of free will.

30 Isaiah 43:19 NRSV.

deep essence of the natural world, such that he could understand the true names and uses of all things. The spiritual experience of being perfected left him exquisitely united with the creation. (In a part of Fox's words not included in the quote above, he considers pursuing a vocation as a medical doctor because he realises that his supernatural knowledge of the natural order could be used in service of the sick and suffering.)

At the end of the passage, he emphasises again his (and other believers') access to a new epistemology, a new way of knowing about the essence and features of nature. Doug Gwyn (2015) describes an 'epistemological break' as characteristic of the transformation wrought in the life of individuals and the community by the Inward Life of Christ. As a result of their spiritual experience, they have access to a different type of 'knowing' than what the world knows. The alienation between humanity and all other species, which began in the Garden of Eden, has been reconciled. The law of the new covenant is now written on their hearts, as promised in Jeremiah 31 and Hebrews 8.

In contrast to some Protestant theologies in which salvation is accomplished outside, or perhaps even in spite of, the self, early Friends were entreated to stay in the work, to search each day for the guidance of the Inward Light for perfect living. The perfection they claimed to know was not a once-for-all experience;[31] it had to be embodied daily. They were an intensely action-focused community; however, their action was never a matter of exertion of the will, but always of yielding of the self to be used by God. It is in this sense that Thomas Kelly (1996) uses the term 'holy obedience' as synonymous with Fox's 'perfection' and with Orthodoxy's 'theosis'.

---

31 This is especially important in distinguishing Quaker perfection from Antinomianism, which claims that, once we are justified by faith, and have righteousness imputed to us through Jesus's suffering on the cross, God is unable to see our sins, and therefore we are free to live as wantonly as we would like.

Testimony

One of the most striking sentences in the Kabarak Call for Peace and Ecojustice[32] reads: "We are called to be patterns and examples in a 21st century campaign for peace and ecojustice, as difficult and decisive as the 18th and 19th century drive to abolish slavery" (World Conference of Friends, 2012: 1). This evokes several responses in the heart of a Quaker: we are proud of our work to abolish slavery, and we are proud that it is one of the things the world most associates with us. It was truly a heroic and world-changing movement, and it is thrilling to consider that our generation is called to rise to a challenge of similar importance.

Yet, if we are at all historically informed, we are also chastened to remember that Friends did not reach easy or rapid unity on this concern, and many Friends in those days opposed and marginalised the very people whom we now identify as prophets and exemplars of faithfulness. Are we, like those Friends, intransigent in our traditions, insensitive to the disruptive nature of the Holy Spirit, using the 'good order of Friends' to silence and exclude the current-day prophets of God?

And, thinking further about our pride in our role in the abolitionist movement, do we tell our story in such a way that we position ourselves as heroes and saviours? Have we minimised or erased altogether the agency of those who bore the most risk, who summoned the most courage, who created the most change – the enslaved people themselves? Have we arrogantly asserted ourselves as the owners of a story that does not fundamentally belong to us?

And yet, this declarative statement in the Kabarak Call – that we are non-negotiably called to this work today, and that this work

32 I will humbly admit that I was present at Kabarak University, near Nakuru, Kenya, in 2012 for the World Conference of Friends. I was there in a staff capacity, with responsibility for many of the pre- and post-conference excursions to Friends projects, communities and historical mission sites in Kenya. The spiritual significance of the conference was, for the most part, lost on me. I am grateful to those who were able to be sensitive to the movement of the Living Christ among those gathered, and who have interpreted for me afterwards what I was insensitive to in the present moment. Somehow, this is often my experience, being an administrator of a Quaker organisation. I thank God that we live in community and can offer to each other the spiritual bread and wine that might otherwise have been overlooked.

is inarguably just as important as the abolitionist work was in its time – does indeed jolt us out of our complacency.

How do we engage with this work? What, really, is 'the work'? The final sentences of the Kabarak Call give some important direction: we must "let the living waters flow through us" (World Conference of Friends, 2012: 1). What a powerful metaphor! At our best, we are unobstructed channels for something powerful that is coursing through us but that is from beyond us and does not belong to us. Whatever is meant by this "living water",[33] it is clear that it neither originates in nor is answerable to nor is controlled by our willpower, intellect, creativity, or activism. At its most essential core, 'the work' is to allow ourselves to be well used. Jay O'Hara, one of the profiles I lift up elsewhere in this lecture (see chapter 2), is someone who does this as well as anyone I know, dying to self in order to be raised up into the freedom of fearless witness.

I am writing this section at a Roman Catholic retreat house in the Sonoran Desert of southern Arizona, where silence is kept throughout most of the day. As we eat our meals in silence, there are small devotional tracts laid on the table in case any retreatant wishes to partake of such spiritual food. Today at the noon meal, I picked up a small booklet describing the spiritual life and motivation of Mother Teresa of Calcutta (see www.motherteresa.org). In it, I read the testimony of one so sensitive to the heart of Jesus within her own heart that she was able to serve as a clear channel of divine love for the poorest of the poor, and an inspiration to millions of people. The way she described the calling to serve the poor could just as well be used to describe Quaker testimony at its best:

Holiness is not the luxury of the few, but a simple duty for you and for me. So let us be holy as our Father in Heaven is holy. The more you are intimately in love with Jesus, the more holy you will become. The more holy you become,

---

33 Of course, we do know to what this phrase refers. It is that which was promised by Jesus to the Samaritan woman in John 4:7–15: "a spring of water gushing up to eternal life". The Bible is full of water imagery, providing deep and complex spiritual truths far beyond what can be explored in this footnote. The point here is that this water symbolises the fullness of life that God intends for us. It is a free gift from Jesus to all of humanity (John 7:37), quenching our soul-thirst as nothing else can do (Psalm 42:1–2).

the more you will be a channel of His love, compassion and presence to the poor.

God is in love with us and keeps using you and me to light the light of love in the world. Let His light of truth be in your life so that God can continue loving the world through you and me. Put your heart into being a bright light. (Mother Teresa, 2003: 25, 10)

In other words, the 'good works' that the world sees, and may even praise us for, are but the fruits of spiritual growth and holy obedience, not the source or purpose of them. The source of them is an utter yielding of the self to the love of God, and the purpose is to be used in the service of God's love for the world. Paradoxically, it is through such yielding of the self that we become most fully alive, fully ourselves.

Mother Teresa described her work as "a gospel in five fingers", an incarnation of the light of God in the service of two deep and infinite thirsts – the thirst of God for our love, and the thirst of all creation for God's love. Our Quaker phraseology may be a bit different from Mother Teresa's, but our spiritual experience is the same. At our best, we can become channels of God's desire to love and be loved. With our "five fingers" – with our full presence in the messiness of this world – we become an enfleshment of the truth. This is what Friends call testimony.

Let us, then, consider further the meaning of testimony for Friends. I always enjoy looking at the meaning of biblical words in their original language, to see what nuances we can glean from this. The word 'testimony' in Greek is *martyria*, from which we get the word 'martyr'. It is usually translated as 'testimony', but it can also be translated as 'witness'. It differs from the Greek word *kerygma*, which means 'message' or 'preaching' in an objective sense. *Martyria* is a reflection of the subjective experience and embodied action of the person who is bearing witness, and also bearing the consequence of that witness.

My preferred definition of Quaker *martyria*, Quaker testimony, is that it is *evidence* of the inbreaking of the Kingdom of God. Or, to put it the other way around, when we are living in the reality of the Kingdom that is come and coming in our day and in our midst, we can't help but speak and act according to the Kingdom logic of love. To others, our actions may seem like foolishness, may seem as futile as a tiny lobster boat dropping anchor in the way of a massive freighter (see chapter 2). "For God's foolishness is wiser than human wisdom, and God's weakness is stronger than human strength."[34] As we live in the eschatological reality of the Kingdom, we echo the famous words of Martin Luther at the Diet of Worms: "Here we stand, we can do no other. God help us." And God does help us, and our seemingly insignificant actions have impacts far beyond the scope of our power or design, and often beyond the scope of our perception.

In the vernacular English of the 17th century, the word 'testimony' was also used to refer to the Bible itself, similarly to how we refer to the two parts of the Bible as the Old and New Testaments. In light of this common usage, it is remarkable that early Friends used the word 'testimony' to refer to their own experience. In this word choice, they made the very epistemological claim that I examined above – that it is not only possible but also essential to know the truth of God through direct personal revelation.

In "The Eternal Now and Social Concern" (one of the essays in the 1941 collection *A Testament of Devotion*), Thomas Kelly writes:

> A concern [in its Quaker sense][35] is God-initiated, often surprising, always holy, for the Life of God is breaking through into the world. Its execution is in peace and power and astounding faith and joy, for in unhurried serenity the Eternal is at work in the midst of time, triumphantly bringing all things up unto Himself. (Kelly, 1996: 85)

Testimony and its manifestation as concern and leading – for Friends, these are the signs of the inbreaking of the Kingdom. They are not the goal, but the result.

---

34 1 Corinthians 1:25 NRSV.
35 For the sake of not getting bogged down in definitions, let us just assume that a 'concern' is a particular manifestation of testimony.

From this eschatological perspective, it is possible to see just how impoverished some of our modern discourse about testimony has become. We can see this even in the distortion of the language – instead of testimony as an evidentiary manifestation, we find ourselves speaking of 'the testimonies' as a list of moral precepts or expected behaviours (Muers, 2015, is helpful on this point). Of course, the 'SPICES'[36] can be a useful teaching tool, especially in Quaker schools where the majority of the members of the community do not share in the spiritual grounding of our faith. In some contexts, it might even be an effective tool for evangelism and spiritual formation, since it may be possible to work backwards, from effect to cause, and thereby discover in oneself the divine source of holiness through the practice of holy living.[37] But for us, custodians of the full treasure of our tradition, a list of virtues or a prescribed set of behaviours is a sorry substitute for the *martyria* of the Kingdom. It risks elevating the fruits of obedience over the One we obey; in other words, it is idolatry.

Conclusion

Why have I undertaken such an extended discussion of matters of eschatology and ethics, of the Kingdom and its testimony? Because I earnestly believe that, unless we contemporary Friends draw from just as deep a well of spiritual knowledge as did our Quaker ancestors, we will not only be ineffective in our efforts to change the world but we will actually do damage to ourselves and others.

---

36 An acronym for a fixed list of 'the testimonies' commonly used in North America. Formerly SPICE, the letters stood for simplicity, peace, integrity, community, and equality. The final 'S' has come into use more recently and can variously stand for stewardship, service or sustainability.

37 Such would be the experience, for example, of many of the American Friends who came to the Society during the Vietnam War era seeking like-minded peace activists and who have become, over time, mature believers.

I fear that this is precisely our current condition. As we face the terrifying challenges of climate change today, the spiritual power required to meet these challenges will not arise from our own creativity, cleverness and commitment. It will not come from strategising or from analysing data. It will not come from ever-more-urgent descriptions of the problem. It will not come from writing and approving beautiful minutes, and it certainly will not come from attempts to make ourselves and each other feel guilty for how we have failed our children and failed God. The spiritual power and efficacy we yearn for will only come when we surrender every particle of our will and life into the hands of the living God – when we die to ourselves in order to be raised in the enfleshment of Jesus, to participate actively in the transformational inbreaking of the Kingdom of God on earth.

CHAPTER 2

Staying low: Jay O'Hara and the prophetic ministry of our time

I want to introduce you to my friend Jay O'Hara, a member of my home yearly meeting in New England.[1] On 15 May 2013, Jay and his friend Ken Ward dropped a massive anchor off their tiny lobster boat, the *Henry David T*.[2] Thus immobilised, they waited. They had positioned themselves directly in the way of a gigantic freighter carrying 40,000 tons of coal into Mt Hope Bay, to offload at the Brayton Point coal-fired power station in Somerset, Massachusetts, the single largest source of carbon emissions in the northeast region of the USA. As they explained later, "We placed our bodies (and boat) in the path of a coal freighter, challenging the business-as-usual routine that is pushing us over the climate cliff, demonstrating exactly what it is we're up against and what needs to change" (Ward and O'Hara, 2014).

As the freighter approached, and armed police gathered on the pier, Jay and Ken explained over the radio that theirs was a nonviolent protest and that they were demanding the immediate closure of the Brayton Point plant. After six hours blockading the ship, and after a significant escalation of armed security forces, Jay and Ken hired a crane to lift the anchor. They weren't arrested at that point, but later on they received a summons to appear in court to answer four charges against them.

On the day of their trial, 8 September 2014, everyone was shocked to hear the District Attorney Sam Sutter drop the criminal charges and make a statement in support of Ken and Jay's climate action. Surrounded by Quakers and others, Jay and DA Sutter stood together in front of the courthouse as the latter declared that "climate change is one of the gravest crises our planet has ever faced. In my humble opinion, the political leadership on this issue has been gravely lacking" (quoted in Climate Disobedience Center, 2017).

As you can imagine, the district attorney's surprising decision to drop the charges and join the movement for climate justice got big press. Later that year, he was elected mayor of Fall River, the city

---

1 During the spoken lecture, I showed the first four minutes of a TV documentary about a civil disobedience action Jay and his friend Ken Ward undertook, because the producers did a lovely job of telling the story in a short period of time. See MSNBC (2015) for the full documentary.

2 The name of the boat pays homage to Henry David Thoreau, author of the book *Walden* and founder of the American tradition of civil disobedience.

adjacent to the Brayton Point power plant. The 'necessity defence', which Jay and Ken had been planning to use at the trial, argues that the defendant broke the law in order to prevent a greater harm; their case propelled the 'necessity defence' into the spotlight as a potential climate strategy. Jay and two others went on to found the Climate Disobedience Center (www.climatedisobedience.org) to support those called to climate-related civil disobedience.

On 27 April 2019, just one month before this lecture was delivered, the Brayton Point coal-fired power plant was demolished.[3] The site will be used for a new wind-power station that will become the single largest energy source in southern New England. On the Saturday of the demolition, the Climate Disobedience Center hosted a dance party to watch the demolition and to celebrate the victory, because joy and celebration are important!

In this lecture, however, I am less interested in Jay's courageous action, as inspiring as it was, than I am in his spiritual process. Courageous action can have transformative ripple effects, as Jay's did, but it can also lead to exhaustion and despair. There are so many hurting and bitter activists. I think Jay has some very important things to say about the spirituality of activism.

There is a paradox at the heart of our faith and faithfulness: the path of unknowing is the only way towards knowing what right action to take in any moment. Surrendering any expectation of effectiveness is the only way to be effective. The emptying of self is the path to living as one's true self. It is in losing that we gain. It is in dying that we find eternal life. This is the spiritual condition that allows us to undertake prophetic action of great risk without ego or a saviour complex. Jay calls it "staying low":

> I am in a place where I can't pretend to know what should happen or what the most effective outcome would be. I don't know. And in my giving over my life, I'm trusting and hoping that I'll be used for the highest good, but under no illusion that I know what that is. But I know that if I stay low and stay open and keep my focus on my faithfulness in every moment

---

3 For a video of the demolition posted by Controlled Demolition, Inc., the company hired to carry it out, see TheLoizeauxGroupLLC (2019).

that's opened to me, I'm gonna end up in the right place. (QuakerSpeak, 2015)

The term "staying low" comes from a letter sent by Isaac Penington to his friend M. Hiorns in 1679:

> Now, this advice ariseth in my heart. Oh! keep cool and low before the Lord, that the seed, the pure, living seed, may spring more and more in thee, and thy heart be united more and more to the Lord therein. Coolness of spirit is a precious frame; and the glory of the Lord most shines therein, in its own luster and brightness; and when the soul is low before the Lord, it is still near the seed, and preciously (in its life) one with the seed. And when the seed riseth, thou shalt have liberty in the Lord to rise with it; only take heed of that part which will be outrunning it, and getting above it, and so, not ready to descend again, and keep low in the deeps with it. (Penington, 1679)

It is only by staying low to the seed (which is Christ within), in unity with the growth and rising of the seed, that we can be given liberty to act. As Jay says:

> For me, I'm pretty convinced that with God everything is possible. That's not like, "If we believe in God, anything might happen." That's like, "If we actually give ourselves over, I can't predict what we can do." … My experience has been that, as I try to walk Thomas Kelly's path of holy obedience, the more I give over, the more I'm given. (Keefe-Perry and Keefe-Perry, 2018)

If, instead of giving ourselves over, we try to act from our own strength or ego or anger or sense of urgency, we risk doing harm to ourselves, to others and to the movement we are aiming to serve.

Jay speaks of several 'deaths' he experienced as he came into the life of the ministry. The first thing to die, for him, was the expectation of a responsible, socially acceptable or lucrative career.

His expectation of a comfortable life had to die in order for him to face the reality of the climate situation. Out of this 'dying' experience, he left his job working for Quakers in Washington, DC, and moved back to his home town on Cape Cod. He founded a non-profit organisation to engage students in climate activism. He was doing 'good work'. But he felt miserable:

> I found myself burned out, stressed out – the movement was suffering and I was suffering. You might be familiar with some of these characteristics. I was overworked with a feeling of inadequacy; I was tossing and turning at night trying to understand what I had messed up, what I needed to do, what more could I exert in my life. I was blaming others and avoiding responsibilities. I was becoming harsh and judgemental, and it was clear that I was on the wrong path. It felt like we were pushing the boulder up the proverbial hill, instead of starting the snowball rolling down.[4]

> This led to my second dying: the loss of hope that all my work and ideas and efforts could at the end of the day make a difference. The loss of that hope. So I quit. I quit the organisation that I had helped to found, I quit the programmes that I had started. I quit my colleagues [with whom I] had been labouring together for three years, and I withdrew. I waited. I withdrew trying to find a way to live authentically and with integrity into the crisis that confronts us. (O'Hara, 2015)

Out of this experience of being brought very low, of surrendering all of his good work and important effort, of waiting in utter humility, Jay found new life:

> Here is the paradox of faith: it is the paradox that in order to have freedom, we have to be willing to give up our freedom.

---

4   This and subsequent quotes are from Jay's talk at TEDxNewBedford (O'Hara, 2015). Note that because this was a community-sponsored TEDx event, Jay held back from his normal use of explicitly religious language, using the terms 'truth' and 'truth force' to signify God.

It is the paradox that in order to be powerful, we have to give up our illusion of our own power. In order to live, we must die.

To live authentically into the truth is to die to our expectations of what our lives are supposed to be. And to die to our ego. To acknowledge the climate crisis is to have all our hope of stability and safety thrown out the window, and in doing so we are given the opportunity to be born into a new life. To place our lives in the hands of our hearts and in the service of truth, in a powerful new way of being in the world. With so much at stake, and so much to gain, what do we have to lose? (O'Hara, 2015)

From this place of deep grounding in new life and freedom, new action arose for Jay, and the lobster boat blockade took shape. He describes how the action was bathed in a sense of peace, calm and joy, despite the very real risk of significant jail time:

We opened ourselves to a place of love and humility, knowing that we were supposed to be there but not having any sense of anger or opposition. (QuakerSpeak, 2015)

Jay reminds me of John Woolman in many ways, and, like Woolman's, Jay's meeting struggles to know what to do with him. He has a committee appointed by the meeting, but they can't even agree on whether it is a committee of support or a committee of oversight. Here's what he said in his podcast interview with Callid Keefe-Perry:

Jay: I desire my meeting, in some way, to make sure that I'm being faithful. To hold me accountable to, really, what I'm led to, and make sure that I'm not over-stepping. [And] make sure that I'm not under-stepping. My meeting at this point, despite my trying to encourage that, is still deeply uncomfortable with that idea in some ways. Uncomfortable exercising that sort of authority and power.

Callid: Even though you're asking for it?

Jay: Yeah. At this point I have not had an experience where my committee has heard a "No" or a "Stop" that I hadn't heard. Or a "Go" that I haven't heard. I hunger for that day. … I hunger for the Meeting, and our Society, to feel really engaged and responsible for the nurturing of ministry. I feel like I come back to this metaphor: my ego is like a Therm-a-Rest mattress, it's self-inflating. I want help in staying low. (Keefe-Perry and Keefe-Perry, 2018)

I have echoed these words numerous times in my own ministry – I need the help of the meeting in order to rightly discern between the voice of God and the many other voices impinging on my attention. I know so many Friends ministers who are yearning for this sacred accompaniment.[5] And yet, our meetings today tend to have great difficulty knowing how to hold prophetic ministry accountable. We are fearful of the authority implied by the role of oversight of someone's personal faithfulness. Jay, like so many other ministers, is yearning for the grounding and covering of the meeting. As a Society of Friends, we simply have to figure out how to do this work better, how to exercise spiritual authority as a vehicle for God's transformative work in the world, because the ministers among us cannot survive long without it:

It seems to me that if we're going to make this work, we're going to have to do something pretty uncomfortable, particularly for many of us who are postmodern Quakers. We're going to have to recover an understanding of spiritual authority. Recover an understanding of spiritual authority and come to exercise it in our meetings and hold it up so we can see it. What am I talking about? I'm talking about the difference between people who know *about* Quakerism and the gospel and people who *know* Quakerism and the gospel. Know it by experience. Know it in their bones to be

---

5   Ashley Wilcox's (2019) recent message at Guilford College is helpful in this regard.

good news, know this core, know this voice intimately, have found its guidance fruitful and have experienced and tasted that sense of joy and liberation that is the Kingdom of God. People whose lives give evidence to that radical reorientation, that reprioritization of their lives. Who have experienced the upending of spiritual baptism. Who have come to depend, to be reliant on God.

Putting people on committees to gain experience may give them experience of being on committees, but that is not the same as gaining experience and deep knowing of that voice speaking within, and being faithful to its promptings. I suspect everyone in this room has had some experience of this authority, knowing it when you see it or hear it. It often comes with a power – not power as in loud-booming-Jay-lecturing-at-you power (though maybe there is someone who brings it in that way) but a power that comes with a deep sense of *YES*. That goes beyond an idea or a notion. When we see someone who possesses it rather than simply professes it.

Recovering spiritual authority is going to take us getting better at noticing when it's present, being able to name it, being able to lift it up, being able to follow it. Spiritual authority is God's breaking into the world, and following it means that we're going to have to be able to tell how it's different than just everything else that goes on. (O'Hara, 2018)

CHAPTER 3

Beginning, end and new beginning: consideration of selected biblical texts

Introduction

I remember when the Scriptures were first 'opened' for me. George Fox used this phrase – "opening the Scriptures" – to describe the purpose of his preaching in relation to the Bible. In 1653 he said, "I opened Christ's parables unto them, and directed them to the Spirit of God in themselves, that would open the Scriptures unto them" (Fox 1952: 152). It was as if the living word of the book had been closed and inaccessible, even though English-speaking people had had it available in their language for over 100 years. Fox's hermeneutical approach (method of reading and interpreting) was to point people to the same Holy Spirit that gave forth the text, which was still actively guiding their interpretation today through bringing it to life.

Margaret Fell famously spoke of the impact of Fox's preaching on her, saying that he had "opened the Scriptures" such that she found herself in a completely new relationship with the text. It came alive within her rather than standing as an objective document external to her spiritual experience.

That 'opening' happened for me in 1990. Elizabeth Watson was delivering the Bible Half Hour talks at New England Yearly Meeting in August 1990.[1] Each morning, she stood and spoke in the first person, in character, as one of the women who knew Jesus. She told us her life story; her pains, fears and hopes; what her relationship with Jesus meant to her; and how she had been changed. It was the first time it had ever occurred to me that the people we read about in the Bible were real people, with full-bodied life stories, even though (especially for the women) we may only glimpse a tiny sliver of the wholeness of their experience.

This perspective utterly transformed my relationship with the Bible. It brought me into a relationship with people rather than with a text. The people who are depicted in the stories. The people who told the stories, edited and remixed them, interpreted them, and wrote them down. The people who preserved them through the ages. The people who heard them told and found them meaningful

---

1 These talks, and more material in the same vein, have been published in Elizabeth Watson's books entitled *Daughters of Zion* (1982) and *Wisdom's daughters* (1997).

in their situation. The people who found their own intimate story within the arc of the grand story, right down to today. These are my people.

There is a lot of material in the Bible that is confusing to the modern reader. I don't read with a simplistic or uncritical approach, but I do read with the same loving intention that I would bring to reading the life stories and religious experiences of my family ancestors. And I believe that the same Holy Spirit that breathed life into their telling and preserving can breathe life into my reading and reflecting today.

It is especially important to me to do as Elizabeth Watson did and unmask the hidden voices in the text, the experiences of those who did not have access to the power to shape the dominant narrative. Like a forensic investigator, I delight in finding the traces they left behind.

I therefore invite you to join me in exploring some Scripture together, to see how we have been shaped by those who went before us in this journey of holy obedience, and how we can be guided by the wisdom of our tradition. It is not possible, of course, within the scope of this lecture, to make a comprehensive study of all of the biblical texts related to the meaning, purpose and destiny of the created world, and the role of humanity within it. However, it is important to mention certain texts because of their centrality to our understanding of God's purpose in creation. I have therefore selected just two passages for deeper consideration: Genesis 1:26–31[2] and Romans 8:19–23.

Genesis 1:26–31

> Then God said, "Let us make humankind in our image, according to our likeness; and let them have dominion over the fish of the sea, and over the birds of the air, and over the cattle, and over all the wild animals of the earth,

---

2 The creation story in Genesis 1–2:3 is the focus of this discussion because of its outsized influence on Christian ecotheology. However, it must be noted that Genesis 2:4–25 offers a second, completely different, creation story, with an alternative positioning of humanity within the natural world, one of service and dependence.

and over every creeping thing that creeps upon the earth." So God created humankind in his image, in the image of God he created them; male and female he created them. God blessed them, and God said to them, "Be fruitful and multiply, and fill the earth and subdue it; and have dominion over the fish of the sea and over the birds of the air and over every living thing that moves upon the earth." God said, "See, I have given you every plant yielding seed that is upon the face of all the earth, and every tree with seed in its fruit; you shall have them for food. And to every beast of the earth, and to every bird of the air, and to everything that creeps on the earth, everything that has the breath of life, I have given every green plant for food." And it was so. God saw everything that he had made, and indeed, it was very good. And there was evening and there was morning, the sixth day.[3]

There are two Hebrew words in this passage that have monumental consequences for our understanding of God's intended relationship between humanity and the rest of the creation: the words translated here in the NRSV as 'subdue' and 'have dominion'. It is necessary to take a very close look at these two Hebrew words.[4]

The first one, *kavash*, is variously translated as 'subdue', 'conquer', 'capture', 'subjugate', or 'enslave'. It appears in Numbers to describe the violent Hebrew conquest of the promised land across the Jordan River. In the historical books of the Hebrew Bible, it is used both to describe victory over an enemy and to describe the state of peace that exists when all enemies have been subdued and the people live in safety. There are stories in which people *kavash* and God approves, and stories in which people *kavash* and God disapproves. In the prophet Micah, we read that God will *kavash* our sins when he shows compassion upon us. In Esther, this word is used to describe the sexual assault she suffers from Haman. It is a word clearly fraught with violence and the exertion of power and will.

---

3 Genesis 1:26–31 NRSV.
4 Although I love the close detective work involved in biblical word studies, I do not have sufficient proficiency in biblical Hebrew and Greek to do original work in this area. I am therefore deeply indebted to Michael Jay, pastor of Raysville Friends in Knightstown, Indiana, for assisting me with the development of this discussion of Genesis.

The second word, *radah*, is translated as 'rule' or 'have dominion over'. In Leviticus, it describes the relationship between the enslaver and the enslaved. In the histories, it describes the relationship between supervisors and forced labourers in King Solomon's ambitious construction projects. In three different Psalms, this word is used to celebrate the just and benevolent rule of good leaders, including in Psalm 110, which Christians have traditionally understood to be speaking of the coming Christ. In Joel it is used to describe the work of stomping on and crushing the grapes in the winepress. Isaiah uses *radah* in two different passages to describe the promise of liberation from foreign oppression, of a time in which those who were formerly enslaved will rule over their oppressors. There is no ambiguity in the fact that this word signifies a hierarchy of power and authority.

So, what do we make of our two problematic words, *kavash* and *radah*? They can't be domesticated in order to ease our discomfort – they are words related to the use of power. We have to find a way to understand the nature of the power that is given to humanity in creation. Do these words, as some Christians today might claim, give us unlimited power and authority to use God's creation however we see fit, regardless of the consequences? Are we to take a decisively dualistic or gnostic[5] approach, viewing the material world as an enemy or a slave, and ourselves as its conquerors and enslavers? Would this interpretation be consistent with the overall themes of the sixth day of creation? Or is there a better way to understand the power that God bequeathed to humanity?

There are two important contextual factors that can help to shape our understanding of these two words as used within the Genesis passage: first, the creation that humans are instructed to conquer is declared to be "very good", and second, humans are declared to be made in the image or icon of God. Nature is not an enemy to be subdued and enslaved, for such an approach would be antithetical to the inherent goodness of creation. Nor are we meant to act as enslavers, for such a role would be antithetical to the image of God we bear. We must conclude that, although these words signify that

---

5 Gnosticism is an esoteric cosmology that believes that this world was not created by God and that our true spiritual selves are imprisoned in corrupt material.

great power has been entrusted to humanity, there is no basis for interpreting that gift of power as the right to cause harm. Rather, it would seem to be the entrusting of a great effort and an awesome responsibility, just as the shepherd is responsible for the sheep.[6]

It is indeed hard to sustain human life within the natural environment. Creation is abundant and fruitful, but also full of peril. To till the earth and reap a harvest sufficient for human flourishing does indeed require an exertion of great and powerful effort.

As I'm writing this, I'm gazing out of the window on the vast expanse of the Sonoran Desert in southern Arizona. This, the most biodiverse desert in the world, is a dangerous place, but one that has sustained human communities for millennia. Today, thousands of migrants from countries south of the US border attempt to cross this desert without detection, in search of a life of safety and wellbeing for themselves and their children. Many of them die in the desert, and their remains may never be found, their courage never celebrated, their hope and determination never rewarded. The desert is a hard and cruel place. Yet, as Jesus went away to the desert to seek clearness about God's will for his ministry, and as the Hebrews escaped from slavery into the desert, people have also found grace in the desert. It is a place that inspires our greatest effort.

I am reminded also of the Turkana people, who live in the most difficult desert environment in Kenya, in the northwest corner of the country. It is barely possible to eke out an existence in that ecosystem, where drought and death are the norm. And, with climate change, life in Turkana County is becoming even more precarious. Yet the Turkana believe that, when God was placing all the peoples of the earth into their home territories and environments, God chose the Turkana for the most difficult place on earth because God trusted in their spiritual and physical fortitude, and knew that they would not be defeated. They feel especially honoured by God to have been placed in this harsh location. The desert is not a curse to them. It is a blessing.

---

6   The description of the good shepherd in John 10:11–18, as contrasted with the description of the bad shepherd in Ezekiel 34:2–4, provides a vivid example of the right exercise of *kavash* and *radah*.

As I look at the profusion of thorns outside my window and remember the terrifying orientation I received from the retreat centre's naturalist (think scorpions, thorns and rattlesnakes!), I can begin to understand why Hebrew words of such power and effort might have been appropriate to describe the human condition within the story of creation. There is a sense in which all ecosystems, all food chains, require each species to exert power over another. This is part of the *goodness* of creation, that everything eats and everything is eaten. By design, the health of one species is dependent upon the health of all others. In the Genesis passage, God makes abundantly clear that the humans who have just been created will abide at the top of the food chain. Such a position will not be easy; there will be great effort required to sustain the life of the community and the generations, and it will entail vulnerability. They will have to overpower the fish of the sea and the birds of the air and every living thing that moves upon the earth and every tree with seed in its fruit.[7] This is a feature of the *goodness*, not the Fall. God saw this dynamically balanced and interdependent ecosystem and declared that it was *very good*.

It is interesting to look at the history of how *kavash* and *radah* have been interpreted. The theologians of the early church understood the command to subdue and have dominion as an agricultural instruction, particularly regarding animal husbandry. Humans are instructed to domesticate animals in order to harness their strengths, to compensate for our bodily weaknesses. Gregory of Nyssa, in his commentary on the sixth day of creation, explains that animal husbandry is a service of love towards the animals, as a reflection that we are made in the image of God, who is love.[8]

During the Reformation, John Calvin taught in his commentary on Genesis that the purpose of all creation is to supply the "conveniences and necessaries of life" to humans (Calvin, 1948: 96). God created the world with a profusion of wealth and resources, and, as a last act, created humanity to take possession of it all, which means that humans are innately wealthy from birth. If any

---

7 It must be noted that this 'overpowering' does not actually include *eating* the animals until after the flood (see Genesis 9:3). The first humans were vegetarian.

8 The ethos of love within the practice of animal husbandry was a strong theme in early Quaker experience, as I discuss in chapter 5, on Quaker ecotheology.

individual person is not actually wealthy, this can be attributed to their sin or lack of faith.[9]

John Wesley taught that, in the hierarchy of creation, humans find their greatest fulfilment in obedience to God, while animals find their greatest fulfilment in obedience to humans. Because of this hierarchical arrangement, humans bear a great responsibility to act as God's vicegerents on earth, representing God to the rest of the creatures through just and merciful treatment.[10] Wesley's concept of humans as managers of creation on God's behalf is directly linked to the stewardship concept, in which we see ourselves as entrusted by God with the safeguarding of an invaluable treasure.

The authority and power that God grants to humanity in Genesis 1 are strictly delegated and come with restraints. God gives humans a special role that entails power over the rest of creation, to be exercised in conformity with the core purpose of humanity, which is to be an image of God within the created order. Does that make us powerful?

For most of human history, and still in many places today, human survival was dependent on subsistence-scale rain-fed agriculture. Certainly, the ancient Israelites who received the Genesis text lived in a marginal and unpredictable ecosystem that required constant struggle in order to bring forth a harvest sufficient to sustain the community. Despite the commandment to overpower the earth, humanity could do nothing to control the weather and remained profoundly vulnerable to famine. This text granting them power was given to a people who felt excruciating powerlessness in the face of the mighty forces of nature. It must have been heard as a great comfort and encouragement.

This raises the following question: what does this text say to us in the industrialised west today, who have seemingly God-like powers to control nature, alter the environment, and produce (and waste) an abundance of agricultural wealth? Who have equated

---

9 This problematic interpretation is the antecedent of what we call today "Prosperity Gospel" – the teaching that God wants us each to individually gain material prosperity. Despite its vast popularity, especially among the world's poor, in my opinion this is a terribly destructive theology that inevitably blames the victims of structural injustice for their poverty.

10 It bears mention that the first creation story, in Genesis 1–2:3, is attributed by scholars to the 'priestly' tradition. It should therefore come as no surprise that the human function within the cosmos is described as representative and mediator, the traditional roles of the priests.

dominion with domination? There are those who would read this text as permission to use all available means of power in order to satisfy the "conveniences and necessaries of life", as Calvin called them. But would it not be more helpful, in our context, to reflect on the constraints placed upon power in the text – our obligation to live as images of a loving God, and our invitation to see the goodness of creation as an expression of the overwhelming goodness of God?

A careful interpretation of Genesis 1 matters in this time of climate disruption. In 1967 a medieval historian named Lynn White Jr published an article in *Science* magazine in which he claimed that the modern environmental catastrophe can be directly linked to the concept of dominion found in Genesis 1. White claimed that our capitalist, technological society is premised on the concept that humans are separate from, and have absolute autonomy over, the rest of nature. White stated that "Christianity bears a huge burden of guilt" for our "arrogance toward nature" (White, 1967: 1206–1207). His conclusion that Christianity has nothing helpful to offer the environmental movement has been profoundly influential, both within and outside the church.

While White's thesis has been rightly critiqued on many points, his charge holds some measure of truth, as we can see when we cringe at Calvin's interpretation of Genesis 1. The western Protestant tradition has played a role in the development of the attitude that humanity is separate from nature, possessed of unlimited power and autocratic control.[11] And it is true that this attitude has deceived us into exploiting nature for our anthropocentric utilitarian purposes. Yet it is not true that this is the authentic biblical teaching, nor that this has been a consistent teaching throughout Christian history. And it is certainly not true that Christianity has nothing to offer in seeking to correct these errors. The interpretation of Genesis

---

11 Corwynn Beals is especially helpful here in describing the origins and consequences of the 'separability thesis', which is the idea that if two things are distinguishable, then they must be separable. From this hypothesis, Bacon and Descartes developed the argument that the soul and the body are separate substances – the basic premise of philosophical dualism and an idea that Beals calls their "worst contributions to culture" (Beals, 2013: 6). I am particularly intrigued by Beals's pursuit of a triadic (rather than dualistic) metaphysics that would embrace both difference and interdependence. I wonder whether this construct might relate to the Trinitarian emphasis in the Eastern Orthodox concept of *theosis* – participation in the divine essence of the Trinity. I give *theosis* further consideration in chapter 1, on Quaker eschatology.

matters in our contemporary effort to live faithfully as part of God's creation.

Romans 8:19–23

The second essential text for our exploration is from the New Testament letter of Paul to the church in Rome. Just as the Genesis 1 passage is key to our understanding of the position of humanity vis-à-vis the rest of creation, this passage in Romans 8 gives us essential clues as to the role of creation in God's ultimate plan of salvation.

> For the creation waits with eager longing for the revealing of the children of God; for the creation was subjected to futility, not of its own will but by the will of the one who subjected it, in hope that the creation itself will be set free from its bondage to decay and will obtain the freedom of the glory of the children of God. We know that the whole creation has been groaning in labour pains until now; and not only the creation, but we ourselves, who have the first fruits of the Spirit, groan inwardly while we wait for adoption, the redemption of our bodies.[12]

This is essentially a passage about hope – what does it mean to wait and work in hopeful expectation of transformation? Is this just a human experience or does the non-human creation also experience a form of salvation? In other words, what is the final destiny of this good and beautiful earth?

Clearly, the interpretation of this passage depends on what eschatological presuppositions you bring to it. If you believe that the destiny of the earth is to be destroyed by fire[13] and replaced by an entirely new heaven and new earth,[14] then this passage cannot refer to the creation as we know it. Many Christians today believe this – that the earth is already sentenced to death. But is that what Paul believed?

---

12 Romans 8:19–23 NRSV.
13 2 Peter 3:7, 10.
14 Isaiah 65:17, 2 Peter 3:13, Revelation 21:1.

One key question is the meaning of the Greek word *ktisis*, translated here as 'creation'. Other versions render it as 'creature', since this same word carries both meanings throughout the New Testament. Who is it who is "groaning in labour pains"? When *ktisis* is translated as 'creature' in this passage, it is usually understood to mean human creatures, although sometimes it means non-human animals, who certainly do groan in labour. A great deal of ink has been spilled arguing about whether irrational creatures can "wait with eager longing".[15] Some commentators consider that *ktisis* refers to non-Christian people, who await the proclamation of the gospel. Others consider it to refer to Christians themselves, since only they have reason to hope for a final deliverance. Some think it is angels, who are impatient with human intransigence. Most conclude that it probably refers to the Gentiles, who await the missionary activity of the Christian church.

Seven chapters earlier, in Romans 1, Paul twice uses this same word *ktisis*. First, it is used to refer to the created cosmos as a source of divine revelation, a means by which God clearly communicates to humans. We can know something of God by keenly observing that which God made, just as we can know something of an artist by studying one of their works of art. In fact, this is one of the fundamental purposes of the creation – to reveal the Creator.

Second, *ktisis* is used when speaking of the false worship of creation in place of the true worship of the Creator – the idolatry of worshipping that which is not God. This exchange of true worship for false – that is, replacing the contemplation of creation for the sake of adoring the Creator, on the one hand, with the adoration of creation as an end in itself, on the other – is called "a lie"[16] by Paul, and it is his way of understanding the nature of the Fall. Having lost the ability to perceive the Creator, humanity then loses its ability to perceive itself as an image or icon of the Creator and falls into the despair of self-regard.

As Timothy Ashworth so clearly explains, the correct understanding of the word *ktisis* can best be found in its dialectic vis-à-vis

---

15 See chapter 5, on Quaker ecotheology, for evidence that early and middle-period Friends were strongly convinced that animals were not simply "dumb", but were fully capable of emotional and spiritual experience.

16 Romans 1:25.

God the Creator (Ashworth, 2006: 153–157). The work of art is not the artist, and the creation is not the Creator, but neither the painting nor the creation have an independent existence apart from the agency of the artist or creator. English just doesn't have a suitable noun to refer to that-which-is-created-by-the-one-who-creates. The closest we could get would be to say "the-created", but this is not grammatically correct. The Bible translator is left to choose between unsatisfactory options that lead to misleading interpretations.

So, returning to our passage in Romans 8 and using poetic licence to stretch the rules of grammar, we can see that the argument about whether *ktisis* means humans, non-human animals, the earth, the Gentiles, or the Christians – it misses the point. There is no implication in that word of a distinction between humans and the creatures, or between groups of humans. *Ktisis* is all that is not God, all that stands in relationship to God, all that draws its source from God, the-created of the Creator. It can be used to refer to a specific instance of the-created or the totality of all that is the-created, but the meaning is the same.

So then, what is Paul saying about what the-created is doing? First of all, the-created is waiting "with eager longing". This single Greek word is also used by Paul in Philippians 1:20. Its literal meaning is of straining forward with the neck and an outstretched hand, like someone straining to catch a glimpse of a loved one from a great distance – like the prodigal son and the forgiving father as they strain towards each other while still far off.[17] It is a very striking image to apply to all of creation, evoking a sense of deep desire and longing, as in Psalm 42:1: "As a deer longs for flowing streams, so my soul longs for you, O God."

Likewise, the Greek word translated as "wait" is intense, signifying a total absorption of concentration in the act of waiting. This is precisely what we Friends mean when we refer to our form of worship as 'waiting worship'. This is a waiting that is active in its intensity, full of the expectation of receiving that which is awaited. You might have noticed that I drew the word 'yearning' in the title of this lecture from this verse, in reference to the condition of intense desire and expectation experienced by all of the-created.

---

17 Luke 15:20.

And what is the-created straining towards and waiting for? "The revealing of the children of God." What is this? It is certainly not the Second Coming of Jesus, for that would be expressed in very different words. Ashworth claims that this phrase refers to the climax of the new creation, when the understanding of the image of God is restored to humanity, and men and women are revealed to be who they are, children of God, "having the same relationship to God that Jesus had" (Ashworth, 2006: 167). This is exactly what the early Quakers believed they were experiencing when they said that the Kingdom of God is come and coming.[18] And they knew that this eschatological experience has implications for all of creation, not just for human beings.[19]

It is a bit surprising to me – but perhaps I shouldn't be surprised – that most biblical commentators do not develop the references to childbirth that come next. Even Timothy Ashworth glosses over this metaphor as unimportant. But then, most biblical commentators, at least of old, were men. It seems to me that it is impossible to miss the fact that Paul uses very specific childbirth-related vocabulary to describe the experience of the-created in its waiting and eager expectation. For me, as a mother, this is a most fertile metaphor. To say that the-created is experiencing pain – this is obvious as we observe what is happening to this planet. But to say that this pain is in expectation of new life – that the pain is grounded in hope – this is important, for it points again to our eschatological hope, the birthing of that which is already breaking forth.

Does this perhaps also offer a different way of understanding Genesis 3:16, which traditionally has been interpreted to mean that the physical pain of childbirth is a curse from God? The struggle and intense labour of giving birth to something new out of one's body that will then have its own independent existence – there is no closer parallel in human experience to the work of God in creation. The simultaneous experience of pain and promise renders the mother exceptionally vulnerable. Here we read that the-created shares in that existential vulnerability. The use of this childbirth

18 See chapter 1, on eschatology, for a fuller consideration of this essential Quaker experience.
19 See chapter 5, on Quaker ecotheology, for a discussion of how early Friends understood the creation to be burdened and oppressed by human fallenness.

metaphor thus deepens and reinforces the expectation of the "new creation", as anticipated in Isaiah 65:17–25, in which the-created is itself born again. Something new is emerging out of travail and hope – do you not perceive it?

And what does Paul say is emerging? Timothy Ashworth argues that, in Paul's theology, the whole created universe will find its transformation/salvation through the restoration of the image of God in humankind. When humanity "is no longer selfishly identified with separate physical existence" (Ashworth, 2006: 167) but is revealed as children of God, the whole of creation will be restored to its full participation in God's self-revelation in freedom and glory. Thus, creation is not a backdrop or set piece for the drama of human salvation. It has a lead role in the arc of God's saving plan for all. The faithful exercise of the image-of-God role given to humanity will result in the-created singing the praises of the Creator (Wilson, 1990: 13–14).

In this way, Paul maintains the anthropocentric focus of the biblical arc – that humanity plays a unique role in God's design – while explicitly linking the destiny of the entire creation to the coming of humanity into right relationship with itself, its Creator and the rest of creation. Isn't that exactly what climate scientists are telling us today – that the future of the planet depends upon our 'conversion'? All creation shares a common source, and all creation shares a common destiny. And, for Paul, this destiny is not one in which the creation will be annihilated but one in which all will be transformed, will be born again as the Kingdom comes.

Conclusion

These two texts – on the purpose of the human–nature relationship in the beginning, and on the role of the human–nature relationship in the end and new beginning – together give us a vivid sense of both our power and our humility. For Quakers, these texts are essential to opening the Scriptures and discerning the living testimony of the Holy Spirit for our right action within the perils of today.

CHAPTER 4

A green oasis: gardening as resistance in occupied Palestine

We want to plant trees in addition to other activities such as a big celebration at the upper campus. All of these activities are to celebrate the school's 150th anniversary. Frankly, the goal is to create or turn the two campuses into a forest because we live in a city that is increasingly losing its green spaces that clean our air and beautify our city. Therefore, we want to create a green oasis within a city full of stone.[1]

Palestine is a place of stones. Beautiful stones, to be sure, but lots and lots of stones. All of the buildings are constructed from the same golden-coloured stone called 'Jerusalem limestone'. The occupation has placed increasing pressure on land use and forced high-density construction in Palestinian cities such as Ramallah, which lie within Area A, the territory under Palestinian authority.[2] The silvery-leaved olive trees that used to blanket the hillsides are being bulldozed for construction of Israeli roads and settlements or in the name of 'security'. There are fewer and fewer green spaces on the West Bank.

Ramallah Friends School has always been described as an 'oasis'. It is an oasis of calm in the midst of a noisy city. It is an oasis of peace in the midst of war. It is an oasis of hope in the midst of indefinitely deferred dreams. It is an oasis of normality in the midst of childhoods of trauma. And it is an oasis of green in the midst of a sea of golden stone. Its green spaces – on the lower and upper campuses and in the Kaykab garden, a botanical garden open to the public – are not only places of refreshment and health but also symbols of resistance and hope.

This year, 2019, as the school turns 150 years old, every child in every class in the school has participated in planting a tree as a way of honouring the past and committing to the future. This comes in addition to the organic vegetable gardens on each campus, the greenhouse made of discarded plastic bottles, the solar panels, and many other initiatives that make the school absolutely unique

1   Translation by Walid Mosarsaa of an Arabic-language TV spot featuring Farhat Muhawi and the current tree-planting initiative at Ramallah Friends School (AjyaL Radio Network, 2019).
2   For a description of the three types of territory in the West Bank as designated by the Oslo Accords – Areas A, B and C – see New World Encyclopedia Editors (2019).

in Palestine and the winner of numerous environmental awards. The creative genius behind Ramallah Friends School's 'green' life is Farhat Muhawi. I asked him to tell me about all of the current initiatives:

> We have installed photovoltaic cells at the Upper and Lower schools and reduced the running cost and CO_2 emissions. Any project that we work with in terms of construction, we are making sure that insulation is tackled, because insulation means spending less money on heating and air conditioning. We are working now with parents and other volunteers in order to do a composting and recycle bins project where we collect all organic products from the school and do composting with it. We have two sites with green trees that, ... if you look outside in the town, you will find that there are only [a] few places now in the town that are green with a lot of trees because of the big construction that happened after Oslo and [that is] still going [on]. The campus is becoming very special in the city of Ramallah. We are going to turn lighting from usual lighting to LED lighting in order to reduce the running cost of electricity almost in half. We have at school almost seven water systems. At Upper School we have a capacity of 2,500 cubic metres that are not only enough during the year but there are left-overs even. And we have a water element at the Middle School where we show our students how water is collected through the roof and going through the well and things. For the photovoltaic cells, one of the most important things about it is that it is educational. We had three aims in mind – to reduce emission, to save the school money, and to make it educational. We have two screens that give information on how much power we produce and how much we save the environment trouble. So basically these are the elements at school that we have that will lead, hopefully, to a sustainable environmental system on campus.[3]

3 This and subsequent quotes are from an interview I recorded with Farhat Muhawi on 17 October 2018.

Farhat is an architect and urban planner who works as the director of projects and facilities at Ramallah Friends School. He is a recent cancer survivor and the father of two young children who attend the school. His integration of his professional, political, personal, and spiritual commitments to the environment has long been an inspiration to me. I asked him to speak about how this arises personally for him and what sustainability means to him:

> How it started with me? I love gardening, basically. It started with gardening, and gardening leads to organic gardening, and because we want to save our environment for future generations, and we don't want to hand them a corrupt environment for the future, and because as a result of the Oslo Accords, our cities in Palestine are cities of stones. Everything green is being taken away and it's all buildings over buildings, and therefore I don't want to leave for my kids such an environment, that is really bad for the environment. … I think, in our case, sustainability is very important, because we are under occupation, meaning: we have to start collecting water that comes from the sky, instead of going to Israel. And therefore we need to, at the national level, to have in the law something that says that anybody that wants to build has to make a well for collecting water. … We have to think how we are going to feed our people in case of crisis, and that's why we have to go back to a sustainable way in agriculture, and go into organic farming, because we want to take care. Sustainability means not only eating good products, but also, it will reduce the cost of the health system, if we provide organic food for our people, and therefore we will also make our health system sustainable. So we need a national plan that can [guide us], because we are a country under crisis, in terms of crisis, what we can do? And, as an example, I'm trying at home to do a sustainable example in gardening, water and, actually electricity, in power, because I think … if we are successful in some examples, we can spread these examples to everybody.

Here, Farhat speaks about the problem of water in Palestine. There's a curious fact that was pointed out to me by my taxi driver the first time I arrived in the Occupied Palestinian Territories (OPT). Every Palestinian building on the West Bank has large water-storage tanks on its roof, because the Israelis severely restrict, and frequently interrupt, Palestinian access to water from the aquifers underneath the West Bank. Meanwhile, Israeli settlements, sometimes just a few metres away, have no water tanks. They don't need them. Their access to piped water – including water for swimming pools and grassy lawns – is uninterrupted and assured. Once you see it, you can't 'unsee' it – you can instantly tell a Palestinian building from an Israeli building by looking at its roof.

Water is just one of the many aspects of life where Palestinians suffer under the occupation, but it is a particularly acute one. According to Amnesty International:

> The inequality in access to water between Israelis and Palestinians is striking. Palestinian consumption in the OPT is about 70 litres a day per person – well below the 100 litres per capita daily recommended by the World Health Organization (WHO) – whereas Israeli daily per capita consumption, at about 300 litres, is about four times as much. (Amnesty International, 2009: 3)

Under the second Oslo Accord (1995), Israel and the Palestinians agreed to jointly manage environmental resources in the West Bank and Gaza Strip, committing to each other to protect the environment of the whole area. A Joint Environmental Experts Committee was established to coordinate this cooperative agreement, and other environment-related collaborative committees were established, for example the Joint Water Committee.

According to the United Nations, this mechanism worked well until the outbreak of the Second Intifada in September 2000, after which point joint cooperation almost completely ceased (United Nations Environment Programme, 2003: 19). Since then, the aquifers have been overdrawn, and pollution has contaminated most of the natural wells and springs on the West Bank. The situation is even worse in the Gaza Strip. Today, only 50 per cent of Palestinians in the West Bank have daily access to water, and only 30 per cent in the Gaza Strip (Alliance for Water Justice in Palestine, 2016). Ramallah receives more annual rainfall than London, yet the citizens of Ramallah suffer daily water shortages.

In this situation, in which the political stalemate has exacerbated the pressures that climate change would anyway have exerted, my colleague Farhat is understandably frustrated by the lack of priority given to environmental issues by the Palestinian Authority. In an outdated mode of political calculus, it might have been possible to prioritise national liberation and economic development over environmental protection. But, in this time of climate catastrophe, such a shortsighted division of intersecting issues can hardly be excused. It sends the message to the children of Palestine that their future doesn't matter, that the adults in the room are actually feeling rather hopeless and do not truly believe that there is anything worth passing on to future generations. The children have not accepted this outcome. The children are planting trees. Farhat is tending the gardens.

For Farhat, the personal and the political find convergence in gardening. I visited his home during my most recent trip to Ramallah, and it is a remarkable place, bathed with his love and attention, a testimony to his steadfast hope for Palestine – the people and the landscape – and for the world he wants to leave for his daughters. For Farhat, gardening is not just a way of protecting the environment. In a land where four generations have now experienced trauma, gardening is therapeutic. Gardening is healing. Gardening is hope. Gardening is resistance.

CHAPTER 5

Unity with the creation: themes from Quaker experience

Introduction

The first time I went snorkelling on the barrier reef off the coast of Belize, I was scared. We were far from land, and the ocean seemed so huge. I wasn't particularly confident with my gear, having had no prior experience. I was trying not to touch anything, because I knew that even an inadvertent brush against the coral could cause real damage. I was trying hard not to get sunburnt or to inhale a lung-full of salt water. Amid all of that, I was not even remotely expecting to have a profound spiritual experience.

But that is indeed what happened to me.

We were floating over the reef, which divides the open Caribbean Sea from the calm Gulf of Honduras. Just to the east of us, the waves were crashing against the outer edge of the reef system. Where I was, there were no waves. I was snorkelling, not scuba diving, which means that I was floating on the surface looking down at the reef and its profusion of life. I didn't need to exert any energy, just surrender my body to a suspended womb-like floating. As I did so, I became aware of the push and tug of the water, caused by the waves at the edge of the reef. The water was pulsing ever so gently, surging and ebbing, and my body with it. The pulse of the ocean and the pulse of my blood felt like they became synchronised, as my heart beat in unity with the earth's circulatory system. I had a heightened awareness of the physical singularity of the planet, in micro and macro aspects – my body and the earth's body became one, a single body of water shared among all life on earth, circulating between oceans, clouds, rivers, and the bodies of all living things. I experienced what George Fox called "unity with the creation" (Fox, 1952: 2).

Quaker beginnings[1]

One of the first ways that George Fox describes his transformational spiritual encounter with the Living Christ is to declare that "all the creation gave another smell unto me than before, beyond what words can utter" (Fox, 1952: 27). This heightened awareness of nature

---

1   For more nuance on the evolving views of Quakers towards creation, see Morries (2009).

became a characteristic feature of Quaker spirituality – to be united with God was also to be brought into unity with the creation. This was not an allegorical or metaphorical statement – "restoration to an original state of unity with God and [God's] creation was very real for Fox" (Morries, 2009: 63). There may have been minimal systematic theologising about this aspect of life in Christ throughout Quaker history, but there has been ample experiencing of it.

The Quaker emphasis on the unity of, and unity with, creation is all the more remarkable when seen in contrast with the developing consensus of the Calvinist movement in England and Scotland at the time, which, in its efforts to dismantle the sacramental system, decisively severed any connection between the Spirit and the material world. Whereas the Presbyterians declared that "no place is capable of any holiness, under pretense of whatsoever dedication or consecration" (Westminster Confession of Faith, 1647), the early Friends claimed the opposite – that all places are capable of holiness and that God consecrates all of creation for a divine purpose.

William Penn describes Fox as a naturalist.[2] So keen was Fox's experience of the integrity of the natural world, even as a child, that he wrote in the very beginning of his journal of his compulsion as an 11-year-old to:

> Not eat and drink to make myself wanton, but for health, using the creatures in their service, as servants in their places, to the glory of him that created them, they being in their covenant,[3] and I being brought up into the covenant, as sanctified by the Word which was in the beginning, by which all things are upheld; wherein is unity with the creation. (Fox, 1952: 2)

In other words, by honouring the faithfulness of the creatures, who remained in their covenant, and by becoming restored to the true integrity of his own humanity through the new covenant, Fox experienced unity with all of God's creation. Mystical unity with the

---

2 In his essay 'The testimony of William Penn concerning that faithful servant George Fox', which accompanied the initial publication of Fox's journal in 1694.

3 Genesis 9:9–17 and Hosea 2:18.

creation – such as I experienced when snorkelling – becomes a sign of salvation.

We can see from Fox's reference to it in the quote above that Hosea 2:18, God's covenant with the animals, was an important verse to the early Friends. It reads: "I will make for you a covenant on that day with the wild animals, the birds of the air, and the creeping things of the ground; and I will abolish the bow, the sword, and war from the land; and I will make you lie down in safety."[4] It seems to me that there are two important conclusions to draw from this text. Firstly, it is clear that God has an independent covenantal relationship with the animals, not mediated through humanity. The animals are beloved of God in their own right, not for how they might be useful to the sustenance of human life. But, secondly and more importantly, the words "on that day" signify that this is an eschatological text, indicating the characteristics of the Kingdom of God. In the Kingdom, under God's reign and authority, there will be no more enmity between humans and animals, so that there will be no need for defences against wild and dangerous animals. The people will lie down in safety with the animals, nestled together with the lion and the lamb. The Peaceable Kingdom that Friends were experiencing as an unfolding reality included a transformed relationship of *shalom* with the whole creation.

The earliest Friends, like many spiritual seekers of the time, tended to believe that the fall of Adam and Eve had not stained the rest of creation with sin (Nuttall, 1947).[5] The creatures remained in their covenant with God, even as we humans violated ours. Friends therefore admired the things of nature for their continued faithfulness to their original divine purpose. Even though humanity was out of order with God, other creatures were not so, in any intrinsic way. Rather, they were subject to "oppression" and "burden" as a consequence of the Fall of humanity.[6] While many esoteric and

---

4 Hosea 2:18 NRSV.
5 Note that Morries (in section 2.2.2) presents convincing evidence that this was not a uniform position, even within the writings of the same Friend, but does eventually conclude that the predominance of the evidence supports the view I have presented in the text above. Barclay, in the *Apology*, cleaves a very fine line on this point in Proposition 4.
6 See chapter 3, on biblical texts, for a discussion of how this understanding of the condition of the non-human creation helps reveal the meaning of Romans 8:19–23.

spiritual people of the 17th century yearned with nostalgia for the primordial unfallen creation, Fox and company proclaimed that they *were already* experiencing restoration through the inbreaking of the Kingdom. Further, they claimed that *all* creation was being liberated from its enslavement to corruption, not just humanity. All creation was being set free to be its own truest self.

The abiding ecological concern of early Friends, therefore, was to discover that true self – to discover the purpose of each creature within the creation, including the purpose of humans. They took a profoundly teleological (purpose-focused) approach, basing their ethics on the purpose with which God endowed each thing. Because God was purposeful, by design, our 'right use' of things must be derived from God's purpose for them. Right purpose leads to right use, which leads to right relationship. It is important not to confuse this teleological approach with a utilitarian ethic, which calculates the value of things based on their usefulness to us. For Friends, the value of things, and therefore their usefulness, was to be found in *God's* intention for them, rather than our own. It is through this lens of 'right use' that Friends understand the meaning of dominion in Genesis 1.[7]

As a consequence of the Fall, humans have vainly lusted[8] for more than they need, and have wrongly used the creation in service of their selfishness rather than in "the responsible and sympathetic utilisation of the creation according to God's will" (Morries, 2009: 83). This wrong use – this unrestrained disregard of God's purpose for each creature – has caused the creation great and terrible suffering. In this way, early Friends found deep truth in the Romans 8 passage discussed in chapter 3: all creation is waiting in travail for the restoration of humanity to its rightful purpose, for therein lies the liberation of the creation from its subjugation to sin. A restored humanity will, through holy obedience, correctly discern the purpose God intended for each creature, which will then allow for a new human–creation relationship. "True knowledge of the creation, and how it should be used, came not from book-learning and tradition, but from God" (Morries, 2009: 28). This is one of the

---

7   See chapter 3 for an extended discussion of dominion in Genesis 1.
8   Referring to James 4:1–10.

meanings of the term 'gospel order' for early Friends, which we tend to use only in reference to church discipline but which actually has cosmic significance as well, as in gospel order all things are restored to their divinely ordered purpose and relationships.

There are some characteristic features of the 'right use' of creation, in the experience of early Friends:[9] our use should be simple and sparing, for to be wasteful or gluttonous in the use of God's creation is to dishonour God and "cumber God's earth" (Fox, as quoted in Morries, 2009: 80–81). Our use should be reliant on God's provision, avoiding any worry, which can lead to hoarding and stockpiling. Our use should be to God's glory, without any idolatrous regard (which Fox, in his Epistle 181, called "entanglements and thralldom") for the creatures per se. And our use should be marked by kindness towards all creatures, avoiding any entertainment that causes animal suffering, such as cock-fighting, horse-racing or hunting for pleasure.

It needs to be emphasised again, though, that early Quaker interest in the creation was only secondarily focused on the ethics of right use. Fundamentally, it had to do with the role of creation in God's plan of salvation. In keeping with the eschatological spirituality of early Friends, in which their experience of participation in the inbreaking of the divine was considered to be real, not symbolic or anticipatory, early Quakers were very clear that creation too participates in the arc of salvation. "For Christ was come to set not only human beings, but also the rest of creation, at liberty through the restoration of God's order. As men and women were renewed in Christ, they not only *saw* the creation anew, but the whole of creation *was itself* transformed as a consequence" (Morries, 2009: 49, my emphasis)."

The middle period of Quaker history

As has been well documented elsewhere (see, in particular Sox, 2009), the Religious Society of Friends produced many notable naturalists during its middle years, even though earlier Friends had not been particularly concerned with empirical study (with the exception, perhaps, of medicine, which early Friends experienced

---

9 Here I am indebted to Schurman (1990).

as a fruit of their spiritually derived knowledge of the right use of plants). While the world today tends to consider science and religion as separate disciplines of endeavour, with distinct epistemologies (theories of knowledge), Friends tended to experience the two as facets of a whole and seek the immediacy of divine revelation as a reliable source of knowledge for both. Morries quotes a Quaker physician, Thomas Hancock, as saying that "none of the acts of any living organised being can be explained ... without some inherent vital energy, communicated by the Creator" (Hancock, 1824, as quoted in Morries, 2009: 200). Thus, scientific inquiry was indistinguishable in purpose from worship – both relied on keenly attentive waiting for God's self-revelation.

A notable example is the 18th-century Quaker farmer John Bartram, who was drawn to the study of botany when, in pausing his ploughing to notice a daisy, he was struck by the intricacies of the flower's structure and felt convicted in his spirit that he had been tilling the earth without understanding anything of the true nature and God-given purpose of the plants he both cultivated and destroyed (Middleton, 1925: 193). He determined that very day to make a serious study of botany, soon discovering that in order to do so, he first had to teach himself Latin, since that was the language of all published botanical books at that time. He went on to become one of the most important botanists of the 18th century.

Observation and taxonomy were of particular concern to Quaker scientists of the period, as a way of understanding the inherent orderliness and harmony of God's creation. For instance, it was Quaker Luke Howard who, in 1802, first classified and named the clouds, which hitherto had been considered random and meaningless formations (Heidorn, 1999). It is interesting that, like John Bartram, Howard was an 'amateur' scientist, meaning that his knowledge was not acquired through the academy but through careful attention to God's manifestation in nature. This anti-academic epistemology is present throughout Quaker history, and indeed it is a notable feature of our distinctive hagiographies (biographies of the saints).

The testimonies of these and many other Quaker naturalists of the middle period reveal one distinctive trajectory:[10] the close study of nature leads one into a spiritual state of praise, awe and adoration. And this spiritual state then leads one into a tender moral concern for the wellbeing of the natural world. Thus, many Friends found a deep integrity between their scientific pursuit and their religious experience, in which the study of nature drew them closer to God.

There is a second trajectory to be found in the experience of middle-period Friends, especially among those who were not especially engaged in scientific study: a deep concern for social justice and the alleviation of human suffering (especially of enslaved Africans and indigenous Americans, but also of the poor in general) leads one to an increasing concern for the suffering of the non-human creation. This sympathy and tender regard then lead one into a sweet sense of God's love for all creation (and also, frequently, to vegetarianism). Thus, Anthony Benezet, a Franco-American Quaker schoolteacher, included this admonition in his 1778 primer for young children: "Dost thou not hear the young birds, when out of their small nests, they call upon God for food? Hurt them not, my son, for He who made them hears their cry" (Benezet, 1778).[11]

And of course it would be impossible to omit reference to the most venerated saint of middle-period Quakerism, John Woolman. While he may be the most enduring example of 18th-century Friends' witness, he was hardly typical of the Friends of his time. The remarkable intersectionality of his work still has the power to challenge our complacency today. He was able to see the connections between prideful overconsumption[12] and *all* other evils: abuse of the soil and animals, oppression of society's most vulnerable people, poverty, militarisation, spiritual sickness, and theft from future generations. He arrived at his testimony, not through academic study or theoretical reflection, but by seeking a single-eyed (Muers, 2015: 180–81[13]) holiness in even the smallest detail of everyday life.

---

10 Here I am indebted to Ross (2012).
11 Plank (2007) includes a very helpful discussion of how Quaker parenting culture in the middle period encouraged children to learn about God through close observation of the ordinary behaviour of animals, for, in so doing, they could glimpse Paradise.
12 What the King James Version of James 4:1–10 calls "lust".
13 Referencing Matthew 6:22.

His meticulous integrity was frequently an irritant to those around him (as, for instance, when he insisted on walking from London to York rather than ride in a stagecoach that overworked its horses). An American Friend, Sophia Hume, was in England at the same time as Woolman and records British Friends' response to his ministry: "If he has this faith to himself, they can be easy with him; but desire to be excused if he is proposed as an example."[14] We may rightly hold him up as a great and venerable saint, but let us not do so to such an extent that we excuse ourselves from following his example. And, perhaps even more importantly, let us consider that those in our meeting who irritate us with their single-eyed holiness may be the ones following his example most faithfully.

It is interesting to note that the passages of Woolman's journal in which he criticised the British stagecoaches for their cruelty to horses were censored from the British edition of its publication. By that time, many respected British Friends were deeply involved in the emerging industrial revolution and did not appreciate the compunctions of their American visitor (Plank, 2007). As Muers notes, the role of Friends in the industrialisation of Britain, and therefore the development of a consumer culture, is just beginning to be reckoned with. "There has been relatively little reflection among [British] Quakers on the ambiguous character of their specific shared past" (Muers, 2015: 174). Not being a regular participant in British Quaker discourse, I can only speculate that this much-needed process of self-reflection might parallel the introspective and confessional moves by many North American Quakers to examine our deeply complicit role in the genocide of indigenous peoples in our continent during the same period.

Modern liberal Friends

I can only touch very lightly and inadequately on the contemporary Quaker discourses about nature, since this is a burgeoning field with far more material than I could make sense of within the limits of this lecture. I will, therefore, confine myself to a few simple observations.

---

14 As relayed in Sheppard (1879: 254).

In modern times, liberal Friends' approach to creation has often begun with confession of failure. Thus, Rex Ambler begins his influential 1990 essay with a lament that industrialisation has led us to view the environment as simply a material resource, and that our religious tradition has failed to offer an alternative (Ambler, 1990). Considering all that has been said in the paragraphs above, I think this might be a bit unfair to our Quaker ancestors. But the point is still valid – western industrialised societies have, for the most part, lost a sense of the sacredness of the creation, and our faith communities have not, until recently, been strong public advocates of an environmental ethic that presupposes an inherent, rather than utilitarian, value of nature.

While it is understandable that the contemporary liberal conversation should launch itself from the ground of "collective repentance" (Muers, 2015: 174), this has proven to be challenging as a way of motivating a conversion of hearts, minds, behaviours, and policies. Britain Yearly Meeting is not the only yearly meeting struggling to find a corporate witness in the face of overwhelming data. It seems to me that there is a broadly shared condition among many liberal Friends today of yearning for corporate clarity on a prophetic and effective testimony, and struggling to find it, and struggling to understand why we are struggling to find it.

Much modern Quaker writing on environmental ethics focuses on refuting the idolatrous lie[15] that humanity has the right to use the rest of creation as it will (Muers, 2015: 183). The work of Elizabeth Watson is especially notable in this regard, as she writes with exquisite sensitivity about learning to love creation for its own sake and, through that love, feeling its condition in both joy and suffering, and being changed by the encounter. "As we work at healing the earth, the earth, wounded by our transgressions, offers healing to us, as to all her creatures" (Watson, 1991: 15). Likewise, Lloyd Lee Wilson writes that the love commandments of Jesus (love God, love your neighbour) compel us to reject a commodification of natural resources, requiring instead that we fall in love with all that God loves (in Treadway et al., 2008).

---

15 See Ashworth (2006) for a discussion of "the lie" in regard to Romans 1.

Douglas Gwyn bemoans an overbalancing of modern liberal Friends, who have gone too far in embracing the "besetting sin of subjectivism" (quoting Jonathan Dale), by which I take him to mean individualism and the overly privatised spirituality of the typical liberal unprogrammed meeting. Gwyn says:

> Very few would wish to return to the uniform codes of traditional Quaker speech, dress and lifestyle. Nevertheless, it seems clear, after a century and a half of Friends following (or evading) the testimonies on an individual basis, that we do need to query and lovingly challenge one another to take our devotion to a higher level. We do not need to adopt rote formulas. But could we work toward unity on 'best practices' of simplicity and sustainable living among Friends? (Gwyn, 2014: 142)

This suggestion is surely helpful, as it reminds us of the importance of mutual accountability, but it remains at the level of the behavioural creed (to borrow Ben Pink Dandelion's 1996 description of the rigid standards by which liberal Quakerism is outwardly performed). How does that compare to the prophetic witness for which we yearn?

As Brian Drayton, biologist and Quaker minister, recently exhorted my own New England Yearly Meeting: "We all can mourn or rage against [climate change], but why is it we cannot as a people make some clear witness?" (Drayton, 2012: 1). Brian begins answering his own question by noticing that we don't actually understand what is being asked of us. We may still be trying to act out of alarm or regret or outrage, rather than true obedience. We know that we are called to grieve, and we can begin to see that we are asked to relinquish illusions that have previously given us hope (e.g. the illusion that social progress and human ingenuity will get us out of this). When individual Friends are faithful to the Light they're given, even in the smallest matter, and bear witness to that experience, hope is kindled in the body of the meeting. "Oh, Friends, remember, it's a miracle that we see unfolding when any of us feels a true concern, however small the motion! This is God at work, the waters of life flowing, the Seed stirring and strengthening as we give it hospitality" (Drayton, 2012: 8). This is the inbreaking of the Kingdom. Do we even expect to experience that in our meetings? And, if we don't expect it, will we notice it when it happens?

Cherice Bock, in her work on 'critical hope', claims that "what is needed is a hope that is deeper than desire, broader than the individual, and that contains the transformative power to change suffering, injustice, evil and apathy into meaning" (Bock, 2016: 15). In other words, what is needed is a fresh corporate experience of the real and present inbreaking of the Kingdom.

Modern evangelical Friends[16]

In October 2018 I was fortunate to take part in a small 'off-the-record' discussion between Friends organisational leaders from across the theological spectrum of the Religious Society of Friends in the USA. Our purpose in gathering was to candidly discuss whether it might be possible for Friends to speak with one voice on climate change. I am optimistic that this is indeed possible – and that this may be one of the few justice issues for which a common voice among American Friends today can be imagined. And yet, at this small consultation, it was clear that the representatives from the evangelical branch of Friends were facing enormous obstacles within their own constituencies. Their very presence at the table had to be kept a secret!

---

16 Evangelical Friends, as a separate self-identifying branch of Quakerism, began in 1947 with the formation of the Association of Evangelical Friends; however, the first decisive departure from other Gurneyite Friends took place in 1926 when Oregon Yearly Meeting (now Northwest Yearly Meeting) split from Five Years Meeting (now Friends United Meeting). See Friends World Committee for Consultation (2006) for more information about the various branches of Quakerism in the world today.

Evangelical Friends in the USA have not, for the most part, been engaged in questions of climate justice.[17] They face considerable headwinds in being able to take up this work, although there have been important beginnings. For instance, George Fox University now offers a graduate theology degree in creation care and is the only evangelical seminary in the USA to offer this specialisation. Its prospectus reads:

> Jesus lived, died, and rose again to restore the whole created order to what it was intended to be, and that process doesn't stop at washing away individual sin. It also involves redeeming the very soil on which we tread. Today's Christians must enter into that process of renewal. The eco-crisis isn't going away, and it's disproportionately harming the poor and marginalised – the very people Jesus insisted we love. (George Fox University, 2019)

Creation care is a growing area of concern for many evangelicals (see, for example, the Evangelical Environmental Network: www.creationcare.org) and they are doing an especially good job of connecting climate justice with other issues of social justice.

I am aware that I am delivering this lecture to a body of liberal Friends, and you may wonder why I am asking you to consider the situation of evangelical Friends today. I am convinced that, as Friends, what unites us is stronger than what divides us, and we cannot accept a 'tribalisation' of our theological, cultural and political diversity. We make a grave mistake when we write off those 'other' Friends as not members of our family, not worthy of our attention or

---

17 Evangelical Friends in other parts of the world are much more engaged in the topic. I would hazard to guess that there are two reasons for this discrepancy. Firstly, people located outside affluent industrialised countries tend to be more aware of the immediate impacts of climate change on their lives (e.g. the Kenyan Friends discussed in chapter 6, who hold an evangelical theology and a strong concern for climate change). Secondly, American evangelicalism is especially entangled in a political situation in which the very words 'climate change' serve as a 'dog whistle' for those promoting a whole raft of other political agendas. American Evangelical Quakers certainly are not in unity with those other agendas (e.g. patriarchy, white supremacy, nationalism, anti-immigration, anti-science, creationism, and libertarianism) but they tend to exist within a cultural and informational thought-sphere in which they are relentlessly exposed to those agendas, making it very difficult for them to hear climate justice messages in a positive light.

loving concern. Evangelical Friends who are called to climate action need your solidarity. And you liberal Friends need to understand the theological challenges being posed by evangelicals, if you hope to participate meaningfully in the worldwide community of Friends.

For those reasons, I want to briefly explain two anti-environmentalist themes in evangelical Christian theology, especially as they contribute to the ethical discernment of mainstream evangelicals and therefore impinge upon the discussion of our evangelical Friends. And, perhaps, in considering these theological arguments, we may discover some woolly thinking among liberal Friends that could very much benefit from sharpening.

The sovereignty of God

As should be very clear by now, our Quaker experience of the inbreaking Kingdom of God presupposes a present and powerful God. Our method of conducting church business is premised on a theocracy – the idea that Christ, as the head of the church, has a will for us, which we can and should discern and obey. So we should be familiar with the idea of a sovereign God, one who is actively involved in human history, in our individual lives and in all of creation.

For many Christians today, the fact that God is sovereign means that God is in total control. Whatever happens, happens because God wills it.[18] This means that whatever is currently happening to the planet is what God intends to happen, and, if it's a problem, God can and will fix it. According to this line of thinking, it is gross arrogance to think that it is humanity's job to correct God's ecosystem, and even more arrogant to believe that humanity is powerful enough to have wrested the world from God's hands in

---

18 Horrifyingly, I once had a Christian leader (not a Quaker, thankfully) tell me that God purposed the Holocaust in order to create the modern state of Israel. An example as grotesque as this one should make clear that this distortion of God's sovereignty makes God responsible for all evil and is utterly inconsistent with the God of the Bible and the Christian concept of free will. Moreover, it is a misuse of the verse "all things work together for good for those who love God" (Romans 8:28 NRSV). The theodicy problem (why God permits evil) is certainly not solved by making God the author of evil and then calling evil good because God ordained it!

order to damage it in the first place. This worldview looks to verses such as Job 12:10[19] and Isaiah 45:9–12[20] to support its position.

Lest you think that this is a fringe opinion, in 2017 a US Congressman said to his constituents:

> I believe there's climate change. I believe there's been climate change since the beginning of time. Do I think man has some impact? Yeah, of course. Can man change the entire universe? No. Why do I believe that? Well, as a Christian, I believe that there is a creator in God who is much bigger than us. And I'm confident that, if there's a real problem, he can take care of it. (as quoted in Gajanan, 2017)

It should be obvious what the biblical, theological and ethical problems with an over-emphasis on God's sovereignty are, but we can't just ignore this aspect of the Christian tradition and hope it goes away. It has enormous political and social influence.[21] And, in order to respond adequately, we had better clarify our own thinking on the nature of God's sovereignty, God's relationship with creation, the idea of evil, the idea of free will, and our human role within God's intended purposes.

---

19 "In his hand is the life of every living thing and the breath of every human being" (Job 12:10 NRSV). It is interesting to note that the 12th chapter of Job was especially important to early Friends in their understanding of creation as revelatory of God's nature.
20 "Woe to you who strive with your Maker,
earthen vessels with the potter!
Does the clay say to the one who fashions it, 'What are you making?'
or 'Your work has no handles'?
Woe to anyone who says to a father, 'What are you begetting?'
or to a woman, 'With what are you in labour?'
Thus says the Lord,
the Holy One of Israel, and its Maker:
Will you question me about my children,
or command me concerning the work of my hands?
I made the earth,
and created humankind upon it;
it was my hands that stretched out the heavens,
and I commanded all their host." (Isaiah 45:9–12 NRSV)
21 See, for instance, Drollinger (2018) for an example of how this theology is promoted within the US Congress.

Premillennialism

As I mentioned in chapter 1, on eschatology, there are various interpretations of the highly symbolic language in John's Revelation. Premillennialism (more specifically pre-tribulation dispensational premillennialism) is the primary interpretation of evangelical Protestants today, and, even if you have had no exposure to theological debates, you are probably familiar with its basic end-time story line[22] from popular culture.[23]

The first thing to happen will be the rapture of all true believers who are alive at that moment, together with the raising from the grave of all believers who have died.[24] These two groups of Christians will meet Christ in the clouds and remain safe with him. Meanwhile, down on earth, seven years of tribulation will commence.[25] The first three and a half years of the period will be marked by world peace under a unifying Anti-Christ, who will establish a world church.[26] The second three and a half years will be a time of great and terrible suffering.[27] At the end of the seven years, Christ will return as a powerful political and military leader to judge the world, raise those who believed during the seven-year tribulation, bind Satan, and reign as absolute monarch for a thousand years.[28] During this thousand-year reign, there will be peace on earth, and even the animals will dwell in harmony.[29] At the end of the thousand years, Satan will be released from captivity and there will be an epic battle, after which Satan and all the wicked will be cast into a lake of fire[30] and the righteous will enter into eternal life in a new heaven and a new earth.[31]

---

22 The framework of the story is based on a literal interpretation of Revelation 20:1–6, to which many other verses are added, as noted in the following footnotes.

23 For example, the *Left Behind* series of 16 novels, four feature films, five graphic novels, 40 children's books, and four video games is a multi-million-dollar industry.

24 1 Corinthians 15:51–52; 1 Thessalonians 4:15–17.

25 Daniel 9:27.

26 Daniel 7:8; Revelation 13:1–8; Revelation 17:1–15. You may not be surprised to learn that believers of this doctrine are highly suspicious of the United Nations and the World Council of Churches.

27 Revelation 6:1–17.

28 Matthew 24:27–31; Revelation 19:11–21; Ezekiel 20:33–38; Matthew 25:31; Jude 1:14–15; Revelation 20:1–3; Daniel 12:2; Revelation 20:4.

29 Isaiah 2:4; Isaiah 11:6–9.

30 Revelation 20:7–10.

31 Isaiah 65:17; Isaiah 66:22; 2 Peter 3:13; Revelation 21:1.

A fundamental feature of this storyline is that, before the rapture, things on earth get worse and worse and worse.[32] Wars increase, natural disasters and extreme weather events increase, and famines and acts of terror increase. The fact that these things may actually be statistically increasing in our time is unsurprising, and somewhat welcome, news for premillennial Christians. The fact that the climate is increasingly chaotic and that there are more and more terrible impacts on both the planet and its human communities is just as should be expected from one type of literal reading of Scripture.[33] And indeed, observable climate change has been seen as evidence of the impending apocalypse since at least the 14th century. The only mistakes, in the minds of these folks, are to attribute these events to human causes and to consider them as bad things. The worse our suffering gets, the closer we are to the rapture, in which all true Christians can escape what's coming in order to watch from a safe and privileged distance.

It should be clear to you that this theology is morally abhorrent. It causes us to rejoice in the suffering of others. But it is extremely popular, and we can't just wish it away. It impacts how people interpret the climate science they hear. In order to respond adequately and communicate effectively, we as Friends had better be very clear about our own eschatological claims, and about both the Scriptures themselves and our methodology of reading the Scriptures that support these claims.

Features of Quaker eco-spirituality[34]

Having traced Quaker approaches to the creation in a chronological fashion, I would now like to turn towards a more thematic consideration. What are some of the unifying features that can describe a distinctively Quaker eco-spirituality?

---

32 Matthew 24:6; Mark 13:7.

33 In extreme cases, some churches even teach that to attempt to mitigate the worst effects of climate change would be to delay the rapture, but that, if we increase our rate of extraction and use of the earth's non-renewable resources, we can hasten its coming. See, for example, the material posted at www.raptureready.com.

34 I note with appreciation Muers's (2015: 188) observation that Friends do not seem to have a distinctive environmental concern, and I especially appreciate her assertion that this should not be seen as a problem. In discussing certain themes in this section, I do not pretend to be constructing a coherent or complete environmental theology for Friends.

Ethical treatment of non-human creation

Particularly with regard to animals, but also with regard to other aspects of the creation, Friends have always felt an ethical obligation towards the right use and humane treatment of the creation as a consequence of their experience of the inbreaking of the Kingdom.

Many contemporary Christian ecotheologians take it as a given that God's primary concern is the wellbeing of humanity and that the rest of creation is of secondary concern. Thus, the moral argument for action on climate change centres around the harm caused to human communities by the changing climate. Early Friends, however, were notably non-anthropocentric (human-centred) in their creation ethic. All creatures, great and small, had intrinsic value in the Kingdom of God, and the recognition of that value was to a certain extent constitutive of participation in the Kingdom.

Especially in the middle period, Friends held a strong testimony regarding cruelty to animals being inherently contradictory to Christian life. As John Woolman wrote regarding his spiritual openings in his young adulthood: "To say we love God as unseen, and at the same time exercise cruelty toward the least creature moving by his [God's] life, or by life derived from him, was a contradiction in itself" (Woolman, 1871: 58). The treatment of animals under one's care was, therefore, a sure sign of (testimony to) one's spiritual condition as being in the Kingdom or not.

Spiritual sensitivity

One of the features of this transformed relationship with the creation – this new experience of unity in the Kingdom – is an ability to sense the condition of the non-human creation. Friends were deeply grieved by the suffering of animals and often preached against it in ways that went far beyond anthropomorphising (metaphorically imputing human emotions onto the animals) but that indicated a spiritual interspecies communion in which the suffering of one was intensely borne by the other. "For how could men find the conscience to abuse it [nature], while they should see the great Creator look them in the face, in all and every part thereof?" (William Penn, as quoted in Adams, 2012: 25).

And it is not just suffering that can be perceived. All creation continuously praises God, and when humans are "turned to the Light" they are enabled to perceive this ongoing doxology (hymn of praise). By attuning themselves to Christ's presence, early Quakers were able to understand the language of nature: "Such as are turned to the Light ... come to see how all the works of the Lord praise him; his works praise him, day and night praise him, Summer and Winter praise him; Ice and Cold, and Snow praise him; ... Seed-time and Harvest praise him; and all things that are created praise him."[35]

. As we saw when looking at George Fox's exclamation that "all the creation gave unto me another smell than before" in chapter 1, enhanced sensory perception, comprehension of the language of creatures and a tender feeling towards the creation were marks of an eschatological spiritual experience of salvific effect. Friends used the language of love to describe their renewed relationship with God's world.

Theological anthropology

When Britain Yearly Meeting minuted its emerging concern with the environmental crisis in 1988, it stated: "The environmental crisis is at root a spiritual and religious crisis; we are called to look again at the real purpose of being on this earth, which is to till it and keep it[36] so as to reveal the glory of God for generations to come" (as found in *Quaker faith & practice*, 5th edn, 25.02). In other words, our response to climate change emerges from remembering who we are – who we, as humanity, were meant by God to be. This line of questioning is called 'theological anthropology'. As Pope Francis recently said, "there can be no ecology without an adequate anthropology" (*Encyclical letter Laudato si'*, 2015: §118).

As Friends, we have a distinctive perspective that guides much of our ethical thinking and acting, arising as it does from the teleological (purpose-driven) emphasis discussed above. It is possible, and indeed imperative, for us to take up our rightful purpose within the divine order of creation.

---

35 From Fox's 1657 tract *Concerning good-morrow and good even, &c.*
36 Genesis 2:15.

It has been said that Friends are considerably more optimistic than other Christians regarding the nature of humanity – that when we affirm "that of God in everyone", we are stating that the 'goodness' that God declared in Genesis 1 was not utterly obliterated by the Fall. This is only true in a certain regard, for early Friends had a realistically dim view of the current fallen state of human society and did not expect people to choose good of their own volition. But they rejected the idea of an 'imputed' righteousness, in which God no longer sees the true person but instead sees Christ overlaid upon them. For Friends, the ethical implications of this are unacceptable, since it expects no actual change in the person but only in how God sees the person. The corollary to imputed righteousness is predestination – the idea that God has foreordained who should be saved and who should be condemned. For Friends, this was utterly intolerable, for it implies both that our actual behaviour has no effect on our relationship with God and that God is the author of evil (having ordained some people to carry it out).

Friends believe in the universal availability of God's grace in the light of Christ. In that sense, all people are 'elect' – chosen and pursued by God for loving relationship. But the response to that grace is not compulsory. We are free to consent to God's love, but we are just as free to resist God, to withhold our consent. To consent to God is to surrender one's self to the Kingdom of God. This, again, is the paradox of faith: the one truly good act we are capable of is to abandon the self in God.

In the argument between grace and works – between the need for God's first initiative beyond the self and the ability of the self to cleave to God – Quakers say yes to both. We aren't capable of saving ourselves through moral exertion, but we are capable of either resisting or responding to the Light. This is possible because, in the thinking of early Friends, we have two "seeds"[37] or wills within us – both a fallen human will and an incarnational will of Christ. This second seed or will is what is meant by "that of God in everyone".

However, modern liberal Friends can sometimes lose the thread of what early Quakers claimed about humanity, especially when

---

37 Genesis 3:15.

the phrase "that of God in everyone" is taken as a statement about humans, per se, rather than a statement about God. The Light, which enlightens everyone who comes into the world,[38] is an aspect of God, not a natural attribute of humans. What *is* a natural (God-given) attribute of humans is our receptivity to the Light. We are made to be in relationship with God, and our essential meaning and purpose are derived from that relationship. As Arthur Roberts said, "Quakers are not so much optimistic about man as they are optimistic about the power of Christ to save man."[39] In this way, Friends maintain an optimism that is not susceptible to the despair of the liberal humanist self-will to salvation.

In terms of our Quaker eco-spirituality, this means that when we surrender the self into the power of God, we are able to resume our place in the order and purpose of the creation as it was before the Fall, and become fully human.

Integrity and intersectionality

John Woolman exemplifies the understanding of Friends that all justice issues are interrelated. As Friends in York testified about him after his death: "He was fully persuaded that as the Life of Christ comes to reign in the Earth, all Abuse and unnecessary Oppression, both of the human and brute Creation, will come to an End" (Gummere, 1922: 327). The Kingdom of God liberates us from *all* oppressions together, not asking us to prioritise any one over the others.

In one sense, this is what our testimony to integrity signifies – that everything is connected or integrated. In ecumenical circles, there has been an increasing tendency in this direction: towards grouping economic justice, social justice and ecological justice together. For instance, the World Council of Churches used the phrase "integrity of creation" in its enormously influential study process entitled 'Justice, Peace and the Integrity of Creation'. This is much more helpful than the previous tendency, which was to see these as competing imperatives in which ecological concern

38 John 1:9.
39 From his small pamphlet 'The People Called Quakers', as quoted in Cooper (1960: 12).

was a privilege of the rich – those whose basic survival was already assured. In much the same way, justice and peace used to be seen as competing imperatives, where peace was assumed to be the cessation of hostilities within the status quo and justice was assumed to be a struggle to overturn the status quo (with violence being retained as a last resort). A deeper understanding of the true natures of both justice and peace has led to a renewed embrace of both, like the lovers in Psalm 85, where righteousness and peace kiss each other. Similarly, the economy (the provision of wellness for human communities) and ecology (the provision of wellness for the earth) are now understood to be utterly dependent on each other, such that one cannot exist without the other. This development of intersectionality is profoundly helpful, as we can see in the example of Palestinian Friends (see chapter 4).

Pope Francis, in his 2015 encyclical subtitled *On care for our common home*, also emphasises this theme of integrity. He uses the term "integral ecology" to refer to his vision of a world in which respect for the deep interdependence of all living things forms the basis for ethical discernment and right action. His emphasis continues to be on the intersectionality of all justice concerns and the interdependence of our material and spiritual conditions:

> Nature cannot be regarded as something separate from ourselves or as a mere setting in which we live. We are part of nature, included in it and thus in constant interaction with it. … It is essential to seek comprehensive solutions which consider the interactions within natural systems themselves and with social systems. We are faced not with two separate crises, one environmental and the other social, but rather with one complex crisis which is both social and environmental. Strategies for a solution demand an integrated approach to combating poverty, restoring dignity to the excluded, and at the same time protecting nature. (*Encyclical letter Laudato si'*, 2015: §139)

Stewardship (or not)

There is a lot of discussion among modern Friends about stewardship as a Quaker testimony.[40] I would contend that stewardship per se is not a strong feature of Quaker spirituality.[41] Stewardship implies that we have been given the role of caretaking on behalf of an absent owner, but the experience of divine absence is simply not a feature of the Quaker spiritual landscape. Friends have always felt the close presence of God, the owner of all creation. Stewards perform a function – fulfil a contract that has been entrusted to them – precisely because the direct involvement of the primary interested party is impossible at this present time. This could imply either a profoundly unbiblical deist construct of a God who set the world in motion and has remained uninvolved in it ever since, or a dispensational concept of time in which we are living during an era in which God is not actively present. Both of these concepts of God directly contradict the foundational testimony of Friends: that the Kingdom of God is breaking forth in real terms, here and now.

However, stewardship is an important biblical concept, especially for the author of Luke and Acts. At least in the American church context, stewardship is synonymous with fundraising, which does tend to shrink the richness of the concept quite a lot (and make people dread the annual Stewardship Sunday sermon). But the concept from Luke is that we are entrusted with all the resources for life (not just money) and accountable for their right use. Everything belongs to God,[42] so that our secular concept of 'ownership' can only ever be provisional. All that we have in our possession is held in trust, for the sake of God's abiding concern for the poor. As an economic ethic, this is powerful. And, as an ecological ethic, it can be especially helpful as we try to wrest our society's imagination away from the commodification of natural resources and the idolatry of material ownership.

---

40 See chapter 1, on eschatology, for a discussion of testimony.

41 Morries (2009) finds two isolated uses of that word in the writings of early Friends (neither are from Fox), but in context it seems that the word was referring to 'right use', rather than a fully articulated concept of stewardship. He does find, though, in a later tract by Fox, a concern for the responsibility to future generations, which could be considered a stewardship ethic.

42 Psalm 24:1.

In his 2015 encyclical, Pope Francis addressed the problem of Christians who remain disengaged from climate justice:

> So what they all need is an 'ecological conversion', whereby the effects of their encounter with Jesus Christ become evident in their relationship with the world around them. Living our vocation to be protectors of God's handiwork is essential to a life of virtue; it is not an optional or a secondary aspect of our Christian experience. (*Encyclical letter Laudato si'*, 2015: §217)

In this passage, a stewardship vocation arises out of the genuine and life-changing encounter with Jesus, so that we see our role within the created world differently from before. But, in my mind, "protectors of God's handiwork" is still too thin a description for our role within the Kingdom of God. It still leaves us positioned as separate from the rest of creation, and it envisions us acting separately from the activity of God.

It seems to me that, very often, the contemporary use of the term 'environmental stewardship' is somewhat uncritical, almost as if it were a placeholder word for the entire content nebula of the right human–creation relationship, for which we don't at the moment have an adequate vocabulary. To a certain extent, this placeholder word serves its function. But because it is premised on a faulty metaphor – that of the absent or uninvolved landlord – I am reluctant to perpetuate its use.

I would suggest that a richer concept for us would be 'participation'. We are called and empowered to participate in what God is doing, here and now, in regenerating the world. God has been and still is active in every moment since the beginning of creation, actively in love with that creation, and actively seeking its restoration. We don't simply caretake or protect on God's behalf. Rather, our call is to discern what God is doing and join in.

Creation as a source of revelation[43]

The idea that the created world reveals something of the personality of the Creator is deeply embedded in Christian spirituality. Paul said: "For what can be known about God is plain to them, because God has shown it to them. Ever since the creation of the world his eternal power and divine nature, invisible though they are, have been understood and seen through the things he has made."[44]

The discipline of 'natural theology' explores the ways in which it is possible to discover the existence and characteristics of God entirely through rational study of nature, without any supernatural revelation. Augustine wrote in the 4th century:

> Others, in order to find God, will read a book. Well, as a matter of fact there is a certain great big book, the book of created nature. Look carefully at it top and bottom, observe it, read it. God did not make letters of ink for you to recognise God in; God set before your eyes all these things God has made. Why look for a louder voice? Heaven and earth cry out to you, "God made me." (Augustine, *Sermon* 68.6)

For Quakers, with our distinctive epistemology, it is insufficient to claim that God can be known through rational study, as opposed to suprarational revelation, for we would make no sharp distinction between these two. We would be more inclined to emphasise spiritual experience within nature as a source of knowledge about God, as is echoed by Pope Francis' words: "The entire material universe speaks of God's love, his boundless affection for us. Soil, water, mountains: everything is, as it were, a caress of God. The history of our friendship with God is always linked to particular places which take on an intensely personal meaning" (*Encyclical letter Laudato si'*, 2015: §84).

---

43 Morries (2009), following Gwyn, considers "the creation dialectic" – i.e. knowledge about God is revealed by the creation, and knowledge about the creation is revealed by God.
44 Romans 1:19–20 NRSV.

Creation as a place for spiritual transformation

In our contemporary highly industrialised lives, there seems to be a great spiritual hunger for something that is 'natural'. One hears numerous testimonies from Friends whose most direct experience of the divine comes from being present with and in 'nature'.[45] Over and over again, we report mystical experiences of unity with the creation when we spend time in spaces that are not manufactured by humans and technologically mediated. For many people, this is the primary, or even the only, spiritual experience in their lives, and it animates a large segment of the emerging demographic labelled as 'spiritual but not religious'.

However, lest we presume that our numinous experiences[46] in nature represent simply a counterpoint to our highly industrialised lives, we should remember that the biblical narrative is full of stories of encounter with God in the 'wilderness'. At all times and in all places, people have sought the presence of God in 'lonesome places'.[47] Fox often recorded in his journal that new spiritual insights came to him while he was abroad in nature, and it was central to his teaching that God could be encountered in wild places just as much as in church buildings.

---

45 I put the word 'nature' in quotes at this moment because, of course, it is highly questionable whether there is such a pristine or naive place. I grew up in the woods surrounding Walden Pond, of Henry David Thoreau fame – our house was adjacent to the Walden Pond State Reservation. I could walk out of my house and directly into the expansive forest and down to the pond. I still love the woods of New England; they feel primeval to me. They smell like God. And then I remember that 200 years ago, they were all cleared for farmland. At the peak of this initiative, in 1830, 60–80 per cent of Massachusetts was deforested. The woods I cherish now, the woods I go to now to have a sense of return to origins – these woods grew up very recently. When the rich farmlands of the Midwestern USA were 'opened up' in the mid-19th century (i.e. seized from the indigenous people in waves of genocidal ethnical cleansing), eastern farmers abandoned their hard and rocky soils for the loamy yields of the plains. White pines grew over the abandoned farms, then these were clear-cut for timber. The woods I love today have only been growing since about 1910. But they are *my* woods, and I love them deeply. I take this diversion to make a point – the planet is a dynamic and ever-changing organism, and I think we fall into spiritual error when we idealise the particular landscape we cherish as being pristine, or original, or 'natural'. Such an idealisation risks fixating on the prevention of all change and can lead us to work at cross-purposes to God's design, such as when we try to reengineer the natural cycle of death and rebirth by fire in the great forests of the western USA.

46 A numinous experience is an experience of the powerfully close presence of God.

47 A term George Fox used to describe the places where he found solace during his adolescent wanderings and spiritual tumult.

Jay O'Hara describes how the crucible experience of his immersion in nature provided a kenotic (self-emptying) purification that clarified his sense of self and heightened his ability to listen for divine guidance. He speaks about how, in walking the Appalachian Trail (a 2,000-mile hiking trail from Georgia to Maine, on which he spent four months in 2005), he experienced genuine joy for the first time in his life:

> All of the 'shoulds' and 'have-tos' have been removed. ... The only guidance that was available to me was inner guidance. The only thing that we have to go on, on the trail, to motivate us, is our inward motivation. Every other expectation has been cut away. It is a lot easier to follow and hear that voice when everything else has been removed. (O'Hara, 2018)

Creation as a source of spiritual allegory

The experience of finding God in nature has characterised Friends' spirituality throughout our Society's history, but there is something I hear from contemporary Friends that isn't as well represented in the literature of prior periods, and that is the use of nature as a spiritual analogy. Early Friends spoke theopoetically, but not necessarily allegorically – they were attempting to describe their actual experience and drawing mostly on biblical language to do so.[48] Contemporary Friends seem much more likely to use analogies from the natural world to describe their experience of God than they are to use biblical language. I think of my 23-year-old son Isaiah, who is an avid outdoorsman. A few days ago, as he was messaging me about a particularly challenging caving trip, I asked him to tell me about his spiritual experience of nature and creation. This is what he messaged back:

---

48 Maureen Pyle of Illinois Yearly Meeting has done some interesting research on metaphorical language among contemporary Friends as part of her work at Southern Illinois University, which one hopes will be published in due course. In the meantime, her *Friends Journal* article on the use of the metaphor of 'Light' is helpful (Pyle, 2013).

I've definitely seen some amazing things beneath the earth. The most striking thing is how a small, unpredictable maze of rocks can suddenly open up into a room capable of holding a small town. ... We couldn't see more than five feet in front of us, and then all of a sudden we could see 400 feet.

Similar with the huge pit that we dropped yesterday. The way to reach it was a crawl so tight that we barely fit. Then all of a sudden you're looking at a hole the size of a small skyscraper.

So there's definitely an analogy of faith and trust there. God's plan is hard to see sometimes, and sometimes the path is so small, narrow, and twisted that you lose hope. Last night when we were crawling through the rocks, I was convinced we had gone the wrong way, until we suddenly crawled up into what felt like space.

And the entrances too, they're often very modest. The start of the journey rarely reveals anything of what's to come. Just a small hole in the middle of a field, for example. Or a small crack in the ground where a trickle of water emerges, could take you to the most amazing waterfall.

Yesterday the only things we had to guide us were small pieces of reflective tape left on the walls and floor from previous expeditions. And sometimes the path was the most unexpected thing in the world. Like climbing up into the ceiling, or down into a small crack in the floor. ...

I find the most reward, especially spiritual, comes from small observations. Being outside teaches you to notice more about the world around you. Often in a cave I'm just following small clues that indicate people have gone through before. Like smoothed-over rocks, or disturbed mud. You have to have faith in the path.

This one short message is packed with Isaiah's perception of his outdoor experiences as analogies for life with God. This aspect of creation as revelatory seems particularly alive among my children's generation today and is becoming a vital resource for them as they face the climate disaster they've inherited.

Conclusion

My favourite colour is green. Not just any green, but the specific and vibrant yellow-green of new growth on plants and trees. I surround myself with that colour – it's the colour of the paint on the walls of my office, and the colour of many of my articles of clothing and jewellery. It symbolises health and fertility. It's the colour of the resurrection, of new life springing from seemingly dead branches. It is the colour of God.

The 12th-century Christian mystic Hildegard of Bingen also loved the colour green. She developed a whole ecospirituality around the Latin word *viriditas*, which roughly means 'greenness' but which is actually rather difficult to translate. It can be rendered as 'freshness', 'vitality', 'fecundity', 'fruitfulness', and 'growth'. She contrasts it with *ariditas* – 'dryness' – in describing the seasons of the spiritual journey.

Viriditas is also a verb, not just an adjective. It is the activity of God in redeeming the creation by 'greening' it. Hildegard's most famous phrase is *viriditas digiti Dei*, which can be translated as 'the green finger of God' or 'God's finger that is greening'. For Hildegard, *viriditas* is both an attribute of God – the one who creates life and growth – and an attribute of all living things – in their ability to grow, heal and reproduce. The 'green finger' is also Jesus, the embodiment of God's creating and healing energies.

This imagery marries the spiritual and the physical into a single green-infused vision of the flourishing that God desires. And, in the sweetness of God's desire, we, along with the whole of creation, can lie down in green pastures, draw near to still waters and be restored.

CHAPTER 6

Hope as an act of will: tree planting in Kenya

When my family and I first moved to Kisumu, Kenya, some of our earliest friends were an American–German couple whose children were in school with ours. Our German friend worked for World Agroforestry and he told me that the Kaimosi Forest was especially valuable to the organisation's research and conservation work because it was some of the only remaining privately owned indigenous equatorial rainforest in Kenya.[1] If you look at a satellite image of the region, you can see the large forest reserves of Kakamega and Nandi, with little Kaimosi off to the southwest.[2] All of this used to be contiguous rainforest, stretching from Kenya to the Congo. So very little is left now, and yet it is still hugely important for migratory birds and butterflies, and for medicinal plants.

When you zoom in on Kaimosi, birthplace of Quakerism in Kenya, several things are especially striking.[3] In contrast with all the property around it, the mission land contains significant amounts of dense forest. The brown scar in the northeast corner of the mission is what remains of the Hill of Vision, where the first Quaker missionaries had a clear sense of God's call to this particular land.[4] The hill was sold for murram to build the roads, and a mobile broadcast tower now sits atop it. You can also see clearly the rectangular outline of the single 1,100-acre plot owned by East Africa Yearly Meeting. There is continual pressure to break up the title deed into smaller units, but, when I look at this image, it seems so clear that the forest has been preserved because it could not be parcelled out and resold.

Yet, when I stay overnight in Kaimosi, usually in the guest house at Friends Theological College, I can hear chainsaws in the night. It is illegal in Kenya to cut a tree without a permit, but dead-of-night tree poaching is frighteningly common. The precious Kaimosi Forest is at risk.

1 Kaimosi, in Vihiga County in western Kenya, is where three American missionaries established the Friends Africa Industrial Mission in 1902.
2 Put this link into your browser to see a map of western Kenya: www.google.com/maps/place/Kaimosi,+Kenya/@0.1916599,34.7988214,55530m. Then click on the satellite box to get a clearer image of the deforestation of the region.
3 Put the following link into your browser to see a closer view of the Kaimosi mission: www.google.com/maps/place/Kaimosi,+Kenya/@0.1279231,34.8432616,3214m. Click on the satellite box to see the forested portions of the mission land, in contrast to the *shambas* (small family farms) surrounding the mission.
4 Their description of the experience atop the hill directly parallels George Fox's experience on Pendle Hill, in which he had a vision of "a great people to be gathered" (Fox, 1952: 104).

In 2004, Kenyan professor Wangari Maathai won the Nobel Peace Prize. Although she was already a national hero, she became a stratospheric national icon from that point forward. She was the first woman in East and Central Africa to earn a PhD, the first Kenyan woman to become a full professor and the first African woman to win the Nobel Peace Prize. It was also the first time that the Peace Prize had been given for environmental activism. It represented a breakthrough moment in recognition of the truth that "sustainable development, democracy and peace are indivisible" (Maathai, 2004).

Although she was a fearless campaigner for democracy and human rights, the work for which Maathai was so deservedly honoured was tree planting.[5] Specifically, she focused on tree planting as an effective means of restoring the local environment while empowering poor women. She did not choose tree planting because her analysis was simplistic but because she had the sophistication to understand that people need a concrete positive action they can take in the face of massive systemic forces. She used tree planting to stimulate the creative imagination of the poor and to educate communities about the intersectionality of poverty, violence, health, corruption, and environmental degradation.

Maathai's work is a perfect example of the truism that the personal is political, or, as the Nobel Committee said of her, "She thinks globally and acts locally" (Nobel Committee, 2004). In her acceptance speech she said: "Entire communities also come to understand that while it is necessary to hold their governments accountable, it is equally important that in their own relationships with each other, they exemplify the leadership values they wish to see in their own leaders, namely justice, integrity and trust" (Maathai, 2004).

Maathai died in 2011, but it is impossible to overstate her impact on the Kenyan national psyche. Tree planting has become totally integrated into the Kenyan way of life, such that it will invariably feature on the programme of any occasion of note – every graduation, celebration, dedication, reunion, visit of a dignitary, or other event. When our family visited the rural home of our friends, we marked the day by planting trees.

---

5   Her organisation can be found at www.greenbeltmovement.org.

As Pam Lunn made clear in her 2011 Swarthmore Lecture,[6] there is an eschatological spirituality embodied in tree planting, and indeed in doing anything of which our children and grandchildren will be the beneficiaries. "To plant a tree is to believe in a future, maybe 100, maybe 1,000 years hence. To plant a tree is to be hopeful, not in the sense of casual optimism but of hope as an act of will, choosing a certain attitude to the future" (Lunn, 2011: 57). "Hope as an act of will" – this captures the spirit with which our Kenyan friends plant trees.

Climate change is hitting Kenya hard. Although Kenya produces just 0.13 per cent of the world's greenhouse gases (Zarembka, 2019[7]), it is experiencing warming at 1.5 times the global average rate. For most people, the impact they are most acutely aware of is changing rainfall patterns. Kenya's agricultural economy is almost entirely rain-fed, and when the rains come at the wrong time, or for the wrong duration, the resulting uncertainty causes not just drought and food insecurity but also considerable social anxiety. Subsistence farmers risk losing an entire year's income if they misjudge the rain and plant too early or too late. Over and over, I hear the word 'unpredictable' used to describe the impact of climate change. The formerly reliable rhythms of nature that sustain human life are no longer so reliable, and all of society feels like it is on shaking sand. This is one of the most common topics of conversation when Friends gather, especially since the Quaker community is concentrated in the 'breadbasket' of the country and most Friends are farmers.

Only 10 per cent of Kenyan land is arable (suitable for growing crops). The vast majority of the country is grazeland for sparsely distributed pastoralist peoples – those whose livelihood is centred on animal husbandry rather than tilling the ground. For those people, climate change is already a life-or-death matter. Droughts are more frequent, and are lasting longer, than ever before. While pastoralist people have a great treasure of adaptive indigenous knowledge, political and socio-economic marginalisation constrain their ability

6 An audio version is available at www.woodbrooke.org.uk/resource-library/2011-swarthmore-lecture-audio.
7 This article offers a comprehensive review of Kenya's energy generation profile and is written by an American–Kenyan Quaker.

to take adaptive action (see Schilling et al., 2014). I see this fact most clearly when I drive north from Nakuru towards Samburu, where there is a rapidly growing Friends community. All of the land north of Mt Kenya used to be available for seasonal grazing, but now, as I drive the dirt road, I pass hour after hour of electric fencing along both sides of the road. The land, for which the Samburu people had no title deed under the colonial and post-colonial land laws, has been given to political and military cronies for private ranches. The Samburu are literally cut off from the mountain grazelands that used to be their last resort during times of drought. You may have heard about this last year when there were several violent 'invasions' of private ranches in Laikipia by Samburu shepherds seeking to pass through with their animals. The international media, as is typical, depicted the Samburu as primitive and vicious, without any consideration of the double injustices of land seizure and climate change.

In Kenya the impacts of climate change are not a thing of the future. They are impinging on people's lives right now, causing enormous stress and distress.

My friend and colleague Robert Wafula described his personal experience of the changing climate in this way:

My cow is about to die on my Kimilili farm due to prolonged drought. She has been expectant and went three days past due for calving. My farm steward had to call in a veterinary officer to pull out the calf from the womb. Everything green on my farm and my neighbors' has dried up and turned brown due to prolonged drought in the entire country. There has been a serious delay in corn planting in the whole of Western Kenya and Trans Nzoia. Land for settlement has been shrinking and people have resorted to cutting down trees as fuel for domestic purposes. The land is becoming barren. All wetlands along rivers have been interfered with by human activities in either farming or housing for habitation. Water has been drained out, indigenous trees cut down. Wetlands have been replaced with concrete for human habitation. Human activities along the river Chwele where I was born and grew up in Bungoma made me shed tears when I went back after being away for over 30 years in Nairobi and the US. The wetland along the river on which I used to graze my father's cattle and play soccer with my peers is now a sugarcane farm and a family home. The river Chwele where I and my peers used to fish as we grazed our cattle has been drained and shrunk into a small stream with no fish. Children growing up in the location are missing out on the privilege I had.[8]

In Robert's words, I can hear echoes of the Hebrew prophets as they decried the suffering of the land as a consequence of the short-sightedness, injustice and unfaithfulness of the people.[9] Robert went on to say:

I have taken tree-planting as an initiative beginning with myself, my family, and my faith family. Each year, at every rainy season, I plant over 2,000 tree seedlings around my home. I supply seedlings to my relatives so they also plant. … While I may not be there to benefit from the trees I am planting now, I have a strong feeling that I am doing this for the healing of 'mother nature' that has been so badly battered and for the benefit of the coming generation.

In the face of existential vulnerability, tree planting is a highly empowering grassroots action in which each individual can make a meaningful difference, and it has captured the national imagination. Wangari Maathai's particular focus was on empowering women to take action against climate change by planting trees, recognising that it is

8 Personal correspondence, 24 April 2019.
9 In particular, I hear resonances with Hosea 4:1–3:
   "Hear the word of the Lord, O people of Israel;
   for the Lord has an indictment against the inhabitants of the land.
   There is no faithfulness or loyalty,
   and no knowledge of God in the land.
   Swearing, lying, and murder,
   and stealing and adultery break out;
   bloodshed follows bloodshed.
   Therefore the land mourns,
   and all who live in it languish;
   together with the wild animals
   and the birds of the air,
   even the fish of the sea are perishing."

women who are most vulnerable to food and water insecurity. In my experience, though, Maathai's message has been strongly embraced by men as well as women. Her approach is community based, scalable and integrative, as people deepen their own connection with the ecosystem of their local context and invest personally in its health and wellbeing.

When I asked my Kenyan friends on social media why they plant trees, I received a whole range of answers, not just related to climate change. I have categorised the responses I received, as follows:

- **Peace:** "As Christians we are peacemakers, but globally human beings are fighting because of scarcity of resources like water and trees."
- **Human health:** "All of us worldwide, the very air we breathe is created by trees. Trees are important because they filter air pollution." "Their use as wind breakers in our homes, they are also air cleaners, etc." "I plant trees for shelter." "I have planted a few medicinal trees."
- **Beauty:** "We also plant trees for beautification of our homes." "I plant trees for ornamental purpose and orchard. It's just beautiful to have trees around you and it's natural."
- **Microclimate protection:** "We need tree cover to prevent evaporation from rivers, this helps in saving water for drinking and agriculture." "Protection against soil erosion." "More trees, more rain." "I do plant local or call it traditional tree, it's a belief that it attracts rain, and shade if it is in the compound."
- **Economic sustainability:** "I plant trees for ornamental and commercial purposes. Wood fuel, fencing posts and timber." "I also plant fruit trees for consumption and for sale."
- **Recovery of a holistic gospel:** "The church has dwelled so much on the salvation gospel and forgotten the gospels affecting other aspects of life."
- **Recovery of indigenous knowledge:** One of my respondents is currently writing a doctoral dissertation on how indigenous forestry practices can be revived and retaught to the younger generation today, as a way of preserving the spiritual, cultural, medicinal, and environmental value of the Western Kenyan forest.

- Climate change: "We should plant more trees so that they can remove greenhouse gases from the air. Trees sequester carbon and by doing so they help to remove carbon dioxide." "They offer energy-saving shade that reduces global warming and creates habitat for thousands of different species." "My major concern is climate change, what we are experiencing now is so sad, as my girl always tells me 'the blanket covering the sun has split.' To her this is the explanation of extreme heat."

Friends Theological College, the training centre for pastors and other leaders of the Friends Church in Africa, has made tree planting, and environmental sustainability more broadly, an institutional priority. Every member of the college community is involved in this work because, from a strategic perspective, the college's leadership has determined that an experiential grounding in environmental sustainability is essential to the formation of a pastor.

For Wangari Maathai, another purpose of grassroots micro-level mobilisation was to create citizen pressure on policymakers to do their part, to make and keep international commitments at the macro level. And, in Kenya, there is indeed strong public policy support for tree planting and forest protection. The new Constitution of Kenya (2010) requires a tree cover of 10 per cent of the land area of the country. The current cover rate is just over 7 per cent, so this is an aspirational provision, although in 1963 the country was 12 per cent forested, so it is not an unrealistic aspiration.

Every individual landowner is also required to maintain a tree cover of 10 per cent.[10] To the extent that this 10 per cent provision is applied equally to all landowners, without regard to the size of the plot, it is considered an injustice by many Friends, since it disproportionately encumbers the food security of the poor, who can barely grow enough staple crops to sustain themselves on their tiny piece of land and can hardly afford to give up any of its productivity.

---

10 It is interesting to note that William Penn required the preservation of 20 per cent tree coverage on every parcel of land in the new Quaker colony of Pennsylvania. Considering that at that time the popular belief was that the forests of North America were infinite in scope, this was a remarkably foresighted provision.

The primary driver of deforestation in Kenya over the past 50 years has been human encroachment and harvesting of wood for household fuel. It is the poorest segment of society that relies most heavily on forest products for daily living, so, until the public policy framework addresses the need for alternative fuels, there will continue to be a perception of competing justice claims in which the poor are asked to sacrifice the most for the sake of protecting the environment.

While the grassroots engagement of average Kenyans in environmental protection through tree planting is truly inspiring, I have also been troubled by a lack of global analysis, leading to a somewhat misplaced moral heaviness. Wangari Maathai certainly operated at both the local level and the global level, and understood the connections between them. But, in my experience, the average Kenyan feels an unwarranted amount of personal moral responsibility for climate change. The focus on the micro-climatic impacts of deforestation within Kenya, while vivid to the imagination and highly motivating, can sometimes leave little space for a wider analysis, in particular an analysis of the impact of neo-imperial highly industrialised economies as unaccountable actors in the sub-Saharan African context. Kenyans feel that they themselves are entirely culpable for the drought and famine that are increasing in their local context. I often wish that the commitment and creativity the *wananchi* (the ordinary people) bring to tree planting could be harnessed to also bring pressure upon those who make economic and climate policy at the global level, and to hold accountable the multinational corporations that bribe local politicians for oil and gas concessions without any regard for social or environmental impacts.

Despite laws against it, illicit tree poaching is big business in Kenya. Corrupt Forest Service officials can still be bought off, and the demand for charcoal and firewood remains high. I still hear the chainsaw in the night. In the face of this distressing situation, to plant a tree is to choose hope as an act of will. To plant a tree is to participate in the inbreaking of the Kingdom.

CHAPTER 7

Fierce hope: the spiritual condition that gives rise to transformation

Introduction

I remember what the existential fear of total annihilation felt like. As a child of the Cold War, I remember that fear, and how it shaped our worldview. And, if I'm listening accurately, it seems that climate change is dominating the psychology of young people today in the same way that the threat of nuclear holocaust dominated the psychology of my generation. My children are having to come to grips with the plausibility of ecosystem breakdown, civilisation collapse and species extinction. They have to find a purpose for their lives, their careers, their education, their relationships, and their future within this existential fear. 'Climate anxiety' is an emerging mental health crisis among children today.

I remember watching the 1983 TV special *The day after* (Meyer, 1983) and contemplating my own post-nuclear possibilities, morbidly taking comfort in the fact that I lived just a few miles from a major military intelligence installation and would therefore most certainly die in a first strike and not need to face the agony of post-apocalyptic survival. I remember that certain death was my comfort, in those days. I remember my fury at the world leaders who allowed this to become my reality. And I remember the jubilation of 1989, the exhilarating victory of peace and the end of the Cold War.

Today's generation is watching films such as the 2004 movie *The day after tomorrow* (Emmerich, 2004) and contemplating their own post-apocalyptic possibilities. My young adult children carry the furious knowledge that their parents and grandparents have knowingly defaulted on the profound responsibility to face the catastrophic impact of our carbon-addicted economy. They know that we have 'passed the buck' to them to solve. And my children and their friends are committed to taking up the work and salvaging the consequences of our selfishness. I am chastened and humbled to be under their leadership in this movement, and I am profoundly remorseful for the ways I, my generation, my parents, and their generation have failed these children.

Apocalypse, urgency and fear

Just as was the case during the Cold War, there are surprising similarities between some environmental movements of today and the various premillennial apocalyptic movements throughout Christian history.[1] Both have an urgent need to convert as many people as possible, as quickly as possible. Both are preoccupied with a fear-based proclamation that emphasises immediate decisive conversion in order to avoid terrible outcomes. The placard "repent, the end is near" could equally belong to either one of them. Both are caught up in preaching fear.

But remember, the apocalyptic texts of the Bible were meant to console and encourage a people living under brutal imperial occupation. They were texts of hope, not fear. A better world is coming. God has not forgotten us. Over and over, the Bible tells us "fear not". The principalities and powers of this world do not hold true power, for that belongs only to the God of love. We are part of a cosmic drama. The dramatic reversals of worldly fortunes depicted in the apocalyptic texts are not threats – they are promises.

However, we who read the Bible today from a position of socio-economic and global privilege can have a very hard time discerning its meaning. The wealthy of the world are very quick to identify themselves with the triumphant figures in the text, and they thereby miss the point that these were texts written by and for

---

1 I discuss premillennialism in chapter 5, so a summary will suffice here: this is the belief that conditions on earth will get worse and worse until the believers are raptured into the clouds while the rest of humanity and the creation suffer a terrible seven-year tribulation. After the tribulation, Christ and his followers will hold complete political and economic power on earth for a thousand years.

oppressed peoples. We need to actively cultivate a hermeneutic of vulnerability,[2] to read as and with those who suffer.[3]

Communication and motivation

The fields of philosophy and psychology are increasingly investigating the unique challenges posed by climate change as a subject of ethical discernment and moral urgency.[4] In the course of my research for this lecture, I stumbled upon the Yale Program on Climate Change Communication (https://climatecommunication.yale.edu). Its interest is to research the different types of messaging that are effective with different segments of the population, depending on what each segment currently believes about climate change. It divided the (American) populace into six audience types, ranging from alarmed to dismissive:

> The **Alarmed** are fully convinced of the reality and seriousness of climate change and are already taking individual, consumer, and political action to address it. The **Concerned** are also convinced that global warming is happening and is a serious problem, but have not yet engaged the issue personally. Three other Americas – the **Cautious**, the **Disengaged**, and the **Doubtful** – represent different stages of understanding and acceptance of the problem, and none are actively involved. The final America – the **Dismissive** – are very sure it is not

---

2 Hermeneutics is the study of how we interpret texts. A particular hermeneutic is a specific way of finding meaning in a text through assigning priority to a starting concept. In calling for a hermeneutic of vulnerability, I am indicating a primary interest in reading a text (in this case, the Bible) from the perspective of the most vulnerable members of the community. There are (at least) three layers of consideration: the characters within the narrative, the community within which the text was originally written/read, and our context today. For instance, in reading Genesis 16 and 21, we would look particularly at the experience of Hagar, the African slave who was prostituted by her owner. We would recall that Genesis was written in and for the Hebrew community during its Babylonian exile, to speak promises of hope to the enslaved. We would then consider what message this story brings to the women and children who are trafficked today.

3 I was excited to discover recently a body of work by a white South African scholar on the hermeneutics of vulnerability, in which he explores the meaning of whiteness in post-apartheid South Africa and the importance of seeing oneself as the villain of the story. See Snyman (2011, 2015).

4 Skrimshire (2014) is especially helpful reading.

happening and are actively involved as opponents of a national effort to reduce greenhouse gas emissions. (Yale Program on Climate Change Communication, 2019)

The proportions of Americans in each of the categories have shifted since the original survey in 2008, with the biggest change coming in the middle of the spectrum. Far fewer Americans are simply disengaged with this issue today than was the case ten years ago. But the polarisation has increased. The numbers of both the Alarmed and the Dismissive have increased.

The Yale researchers then developed messaging strategies to address the specific conditions of each of the six audience segments.[5] The full details of their work, and the lessons we might draw from it in our own activism, are beyond the scope of this lecture. The point I wish to emphasise by mentioning this fascinating research is that it provides us with an important psychological and spiritual reminder. People's abilities to receive and process new information, and make changes in their lives, are very much circumscribed by their current spiritual condition. And too many of the communication efforts of climate activists are falling on deaf ears – or, worse, having the opposite effect.

Fear is rarely a good motivator, even though those in the Alarmed segment can be tempted by an urgent need to provoke fear in those who are complacent. I am absolutely convinced that people can't access imaginative positive futures – prophetic imagination – when they start from a place of fear, scarcity, threat, and guilt (although they are fully capable of imagining all kinds of catastrophically negative futures). In particular, the fear of loss is highly paralysing.

---

5   For instance, the Alarmed and Concerned audiences need to be given information about effective action they can take. The Alarmed are also receptive to information about how they can be more effective opinion leaders in their communities. The Cautious and Disengaged audiences are not likely to process any fact-based appeal but are receptive to stories and might best be reached through movies, novels, video games, and other entertainment media. These groups are also the most receptive to social norms and so are open to being shaped by the behaviour of others. The Doubtful and the Dismissive audiences actively believe that climate change is either not real or not a problem. They are likely to reject direct messaging to the contrary, seeing it as politically biased. But they may be receptive to messages that build on their core values, such as emphasising solutions that do not involve government regulation. The research itself doesn't give this example, but it seems to me that one way to find common ground with evangelical Friends is through our shared concern for the impact of severe weather events on the world's most vulnerable populations.

When we focus our messaging on what will be lost as the climate changes, we risk people being unable to respond to that information. Fear and scarcity short-circuit the brain in ways that isolate us from our own hope and creativity. And there's an increasing body of psychological research that supports the idea that dire warnings and fear-provoking messages backfire with the so-called boomerang effect, making people *less* likely to take action (Feinberg and Willer, 2011; Reser and Bradley, 2017).

This means it is problematic when we start our communication with a problem statement, yet we do this over and over again. Our statements on climate change begin with recitations of doom, fact after fact after terrifying fact. I don't think this convinces anyone who wasn't already on board, and, as Jay O'Hara (2015) testified, frenetically trying to provoke others is a sure recipe for despair.

So, if scare tactics don't motivate, what does? The answer is hope. And creative alternatives. And the vision of a better future. And the message that each one of us can make a meaningful difference. Examples of other people taking action (van der Linden et al., 2015). The research shows that facts coupled with invitations to concrete action are much more effective than facts alone. Or, as your own Laurie Michaelis so rightly said, "persuasion rarely works, but living our values can be contagious" (Michaelis, 2017: 22). As we ourselves surrender to participation in the Kingdom, our lives will preach more effectively than our words alone.

Prophetic imagination

If we're not preaching fear, does that mean we're avoiding telling the truth about the existential threat we face? Are we soft-pedalling in order to avoid upsetting people? I certainly hope not. Fear is an important element in the range of our human experience, especially as it points us to the truth. If I'm counselling us not to dwell in fear, what am I offering instead, as a response to our genuinely terrifying reality?

My dear friend Welling Hall, a Quaker, a political scientist and an artist, is called to a ministry of making what she calls "political art". She works in various media in order to give shape and expression to the horror of violence, finding, as she does so, that "the best antidote to horror is intense aesthetic engagement" (Ashley and Hall, 2018). Imagination and creativity are some of our most powerful access points for allowing God's living water to flow through us with holy urgency.

Walter Brueggemann, a Hebrew Bible scholar and influential writer on the 'prophetic imagination', points us to the experience of the Israelites crying out under the oppression of slavery:[6]

> In the verb 'cry out' (za'ak)[7] there is a bit of ambiguity because on the one hand it is a cry of misery and wretchedness with some self-pity, while it also functions for the official filing of a legal complaint. The mournful one is the plaintiff. … The grieving of Israel – perhaps self-pity and surely complaint but never resignation – is the beginning of criticism. It is made clear that things are not as they should be, not as they were promised, and not as they must be and will be. (Brueggemann, 2001: 11–12)

And God hears our cry.[8] God joins us in our yearning for liberation. This double cry – the cry of lament for injustice and the cry of the struggle for freedom – is met again in the Romans 8 passage in which all creation is crying out for liberation.

I wonder whether we have lost the ability to cry out, to grieve with prophetic impact. Many cultures have rituals and customs for embodying grief, thereby allowing the body to metabolise it. But, in the predominantly white, middle-class culture of Anglo-American Quakerism, we don't seem to know what to do with grief. We don't allow ourselves to experience the depth of our lament, because such raw and physical emotion might make someone uncomfortable. Have we yet allowed ourselves to feel the condition of our children? Have we, like Rachel, wept for our children and their children?[9]

---

6 Exodus 2:23.
7 Za'ak is how Brueggemann renders the Hebrew word in his book, but that spelling is normally reserved for a different Hebrew word, Strong's Number 2193. The word Brueggemann is discussing is Strong's Number 2199, and is usually rendered as za'aq. ('Strong's Concordance' is an exhaustive numbered list of every Greek and Hebrew word in the Bible.)
8 Exodus 2:24–25, 3:7–10.
9 Jeremiah 31:15; Matthew 2:18.

Early Friend Mary Howgill, in 1662, gave voice to the deep sorrow she felt, and how it manifested in her body, upon coming to an understanding of the injustice of the English class system:

Then did sorrow seize on my heart, and great grief upon my soul, and a great weight upon my body, which caused my lips to quiver, and my belly to tremble, and a Cry ran through me, O Lord, what wilt thou do with the Land, or with thy People therein, unto whom thou hast so largely manifested thy Name? ... Then the Cry was in me, O Lord, slay not the Righteous with the Wicked: And a great Earthquake was upon me, and I was in great travail in spirit, soul, and body, for the whole Land of England, and little or no comfort had I, until I heard the Lord's voice, who spake unto me, and said, Fear not thou, my Daughter, none of these things which I have shewed unto thee; but believe in my Name, made known unto thee. Then I said, O Lord, who shall stand for thee? (Howgill, 1662)

In this passage, Howgill describes the movement from conviction to desolation to consolation to action, as she cried out to God and her cry was heard.

I often said to people, during the years I lived in Kenya and facilitated Quaker visitors to various Kenyan Quaker ministries, that "if you're not broken-hearted, you're not paying attention". I didn't encourage broken-heartedness because I wanted to crush people with guilt or fear, but because it is out of being broken that we can become useful to God. For, as we are reminded in Psalm 51, "the sacrifice acceptable to God is a broken spirit; a broken and contrite heart, O God, you will not despise".[10]

When fear and anger move through grief and lament and into broken-heartedness and contrition, then, like empty vessels, can we become clear channels for participation in God's inbreaking Kingdom. We can embody an alternative vision of reality. Then, the prophetic ministry of "fearless truth-telling together with fierce

---

10 Psalm 51:17.

hope"[11] emerges, as it did for Jay O'Hara and has for so many others – not as an act of duty or will, but as a bursting forth of freedom, joy and peace. This is what is meant by 'holy obedience', testimony and participation in the Kingdom of God.

The danger of depletion

My son's partner, Heather, is an environmental engineer, and she told me something that has stayed with me as an analogy and as a caution about my spiritual condition. I love water as a spiritual medium and I am always drawn to water metaphors. As I've been struggling with burnout over the past couple of years, I've been using the metaphor of a dry well. I've felt bone dry and completely depleted in my ministry. During my sabbatical from Friends United Meeting over the past two months, my goal has been to replenish the deep, cool, life-giving waters of the well, to allow the water to seep in from hidden depths and rise up with fresh life. I want to feel full again, full of the water of life that Jesus promises to the outcast woman at the well.[12]

But Heather told me about what happens when natural underground aquifers are overharvested. She told me about the aquifer under the Central Valley in California, where the extraction of water for urban and agricultural use routinely exceeds its natural recharge rate. Over time, as the aquifer is drained, the land actually sinks. The water was holding up the ground, but a vacant cavity can't do that. This is called 'land subsidence', and it is a problem in many places around the world. The Central Valley has sunk by as much as eight and a half metres in 100 years.

The thing that Heather told me that really brought me up short was that the subsidence is permanent. Even if we were to stop overdrawing the aquifer, even if there were abundant snow pack in the mountains and the Central Valley were completely re-watered, the land wouldn't re-elevate. The cavity wouldn't re-expand. The

---

11 I believe these words are Krista Tippett's, from her conversation with Walter Brueggemann on the radio show *On Being* on 22 December 2011. However, they may actually be Brueggemann's words, for which I cannot find a precise citation. See Tippett (2011).

12 John 4:7–42.

aquifer will never again hold the capacity of water it used to. The damage is permanent.

I think we are more like the aquifer than the well. Repeated unsustainable cycles of overharvesting cause permanent damage to our souls. Burnout, recovery, burnout, recovery – this is no way to live! Just as we need to maintain a sustainable balance between harvesting and refilling the aquifer, we need to maintain a sustainable balance of spiritual inputs and outflows in our lives.

What, then, shall we do?

Climate justice is overwhelming work. The sheer scale of the transition we need to make as a human community can dwarf our seemingly inadequate personal responses, and we can be tempted to feel like the only moral thing to do is to work harder and harder and harder. But if we try to work harder by drawing on our own resources, by extracting everything we can from our spiritual aquifer, we will do damage to ourselves. It is only by letting the living waters flow freely through us that we can stay in the work in a healthy and joyful way.

How do we do this? How do we let the living waters flow through us? What should we be doing?

I don't have answers to those questions for each Friend and community of Friends in their context. But I do know that this advice helps: do the one thing that only you can do, that God has uniquely created you to do, that feels like it is smack dab in the centre of God's will and purpose and love for you. You might doubt that it is important, or that it is enough. But take comfort in knowing that God has also called everyone else to do their unique thing. You don't need to feel responsible for the whole. Give up needing to see the big picture of how it all fits together.

How do you know what God has uniquely created and prepared you to do? I'm convinced that this discernment isn't as hard as it sounds, because God *wants* to guide and direct you. God isn't playing hide-and-seek in your life. You can trust the guidance you feel. Follow your passion and joy. Notice the moments when you feel most deeply alive, most profoundly plugged in to the electric energy of the Holy Spirit. Trust that, if you are centring your heart on God, the desires of your heart will guide you rightly. When you are walking in the centre of God's purpose for you, the work may be hard, but it will also be joyful. It will probably also be scary or risky, but test whether you see evidence of the Fruits of the Spirit[13] growing day by day in your life. If you do, you're on the right track. If, instead, you discover those *other* fruits[14] (as Jay did when he realised he was burning out on 'good works'), then step back and recentre in God.

Don't try to do this alone. We need the accountability of the spiritual community, for them to walk with us in prayer and discernment. We need counsel, to see what is right in front of us. We need companionship in the path of holy obedience. As Jay said, our egos are self-inflating. Stay low, stay together, fearlessly do the foolish thing, and expect that your life will be evidence of the miraculous.[15]

Conclusion

When I visited Belize a couple of months ago, I had the opportunity to go 'cave tubing', which was a new experience for me. Our group clambered and scrambled far up into a cave in a mountain on the border with Guatemala, each one of us awkwardly carrying a large inner tube the whole way. We hadn't gone very far inside the cave before we'd exhausted the reach of the daylight, and the lamps on our helmets were the only source of light to guide the way. It was at times steep, at times slippery, at times a tight squeeze, especially for someone with a larger body, like me. Eventually, we reached a pool of water.

Our guide instructed us in how to recline in the tube in the water. It felt a bit awkward at first, but, with some coaching and a bit of adjustment, I was able to find a comfortable position. And then, once everyone in our group was settled in their tube, our guide told us to switch off our lamps.

---

13 Galatians 5:22–23.
14 Galatians 5:19–21. (In our world today, I would add 'virtue signalling' to Paul's list of the works of the flesh.)
15 See chapter 2.

The dark was absolute, even darker than the darkest night sky, which still carries some hint of starlight within it. This darkness was enveloping and disorienting. It was, at first, rather frightening. There was no way to know which direction I was facing, or whether I was heading towards a collision with a boulder or another tuber. I tried to exert some kind of control, to peer into the darkness for any clues that could orient me and help me steer my tube. But that was pointless.

And so I relaxed. I stopped trying to do anything, and just surrendered to the water. It didn't matter whether my eyes were open or closed, for there was nothing to see. Instead, I felt the water. I felt the current of the underground river, moving inexorably towards the sea. I felt the movement of the earth around the sun. I felt myself in both absolute stillness and constant motion. I allowed the power of the water to overwhelm my feeble attempts at power and control, and I surrendered my will. In this transcendent state, I floated downstream. I had no ability to perceive time or distance or orientation or context, but I was overwhelmed with a sensation of trust. The current of the river was utterly trustworthy. There was zero risk that it would carry me into a dead end. I would, inevitably, emerge into the light. All that was required of me in that moment was to yield to its current.

Not long ago, I stumbled upon a small booklet of the writings of Rumi, a 13th-century Sufi mystic. Among the many treasures I discovered, there was this small gem: God loves us like "an ocean wooing a drop" (Rumi, *Mathnawi IV*, lines 2916–2922). An ocean wooing a drop! What tender love the ocean has for that tiny drop! Despite all the other drops in the universe, what lengths the ocean goes to, to find and woo that one drop. And as for me – the tiny drop, the powerless speck – all that I have to do, all that God asks of me, is to give my consent. To say yes to the power and love of the ocean, to be propelled onward as an instrument of the Ocean of Light that is already, right now, transforming the world.

REFLECTING ON AND ENGAGING WITH THE LECTURE

The Swarthmore Lecture Committee has designed the following activities to help Friends explore and reflect on this year's lecture.

Using these activities

Although the guidelines are quite strict, the activities are designed to be used very flexibly. There are activities for individuals, small groups (twos, threes or fours) and larger groups (with a focus on whole meetings).

The activities have been designed to be done with minimal equipment. Participants may wish to bring pens and paper or notebooks for their own notes. Where equipment is needed, this is specified.

Although the activities are divided into seven sections, each relating to a different chapter of the book, you may wish to spread them over more sessions, going at a pace that suits the group. It is recommended that each session runs for a maximum of 90 minutes.

Guidance for facilitators and group members

In undertaking these activities, it is important that all participants come with heart and mind prepared. It would probably be helpful for some members of each group to be designated as 'facilitators', perhaps on a rotating basis, to guide the group through the process, keep an eye on time and 'hold' the group. It may be appropriate for them to decide the order in which the group approaches the activities, the methods used and the framework in which the group will work. Everyone else should not come expecting to be directed or merely guided through the process but should engage fully and wholeheartedly. As Friends, we do not have a separated priesthood, and all have the clergy's responsibility for the maintenance of the meeting as a community. Similarly, in our groups, we all hold the responsibility to work collaboratively in order for the group to work together, enabling us to reflect on our spiritual journeys and helping us to see the Light in our lives, and in the community in which we worship together.

Discuss and agree how the group will work together

In small groups and whole meeting groups, all members of the group should have a chance to share, and one or two persons should not dominate the spoken contributions (this includes the facilitators). It may be helpful to state a few general guidelines, which are the foundation for the approaches below:

- **Come to the group with as much of ourselves as possible.** This means two things: to be as present as we can be (which may differ depending on the day, or the time of day or what else is happening) and to bring all of who we are – our joys and successes, our fears and failings. You may pass if you do not wish to speak to the topic or answer a question.
- **Presume welcome and extend welcome.** We support each other's participation and growth by giving and receiving hospitality.
- **No fixing.** No fixing, counselling or setting straight. Facilitators and fellow participants should support each other rather than try to set each other straight.
- **When the going gets tough, turn to wonder.** When you find yourself reacting harshly, disagreeing with another, becoming judgemental or becoming defensive, ask questions such as, "I wonder what my reaction teaches me about myself."
- **Speak for self.** Using 'I' statements, speak your truth in a way that respects the truths of others. Speak for a second time only after others have had a chance to speak once.
- **Listen with 'soft eyes'.** Listen to others with eyes of compassion and understanding.
- **Trust and learn from silence.** Silence is a rare gift in our busy world. Allow silence to be another member of the group. Leave silence between speakers.
- **Observe confidentiality.** The main issue in relation to confidentiality is how agreeing exceptions will work in practice.

There will be times when people share ideas, approaches or experiences that are helpful to others. It is part of our Quaker tradition that we share and learn from each other within the priesthood of all believers. However, it is important to respect individuals' personal stories. A general principle is that it is okay to share ideas but not personal stories. The following is a suggestion that you can adapt to suit your group:

- Everything shared in pairs and small groups is confidential to those present *except for* agreed things, which may be reported to the main group and discussed during the session.
- Everything shared in the whole group stays in the group and is not discussed outside the session *except for* agreed things, which may be discussed outside the session between course members only.

- **Accept imperfection.** In ourselves and in others.

Approaches for group work

Creative listening[1]
Participants take turns around the circle, giving each person a chance to say something on the topic. Limiting the responses to two or three minutes may be useful so that the entire time is not used in this one go-round.

- Each offering is given without expectation of questions or comments from others in the group.
- To help share time equally, a watch may be held by the person who has just spoken and handed to the next speaker at the end of the allotted time.

Creative listening may also be used for longer contributions, in which case people may contribute in any order. Two suggestions to encourage equal participation are:

- **Talking stick.** An object, such as a shell, smooth pebble or pine

---

1   Adapted with permission from *Hearts & minds prepared facilitator handbook*, published by Woodbrooke Quaker Study Centre, 2003.

cone, is picked up by a speaker, who must not be interrupted while holding it. The object can be picked up by anyone for their turn after it has been replaced in the centre of the circle. Some Native North American groups call it the 'talking stick'. This method is usually most effective when linked with periods of silent worship in between contributions.

- **Stones or tokens.** Try giving two or three stones or other small objects to each person, each 'worth' two minutes. After a minute or so at the start, anyone may toss one into the middle of the circle to signify that they are ready to use the next two minutes of the group's time. A timekeeper can be used. As in the 'go-round', no comments or questions should be allowed to follow the offerings.

Worship sharing

This can be particularly suitable for potentially controversial, difficult or personal topics. It differs from creative listening in that it is based less on thinking than on surrendering ourselves to worship and accepting what emerges. Although participants are asked to reflect on the questions in advance, contributions are likely to be at a deeper level, sometimes surprising to the speakers themselves. Here, it is usually best to state the question or issue, and then start with a short period of silence (about five minutes) in which each person moves into worship and thinks of the contribution they may feel called to make. People then speak in any order. Close with a period of silent worship.

- The emphasis is on worshipful listening.
- The group may agree before starting to place time limitations on each person so that everyone has a chance to speak. In this case, if one person is approaching the time limit, the facilitator should intervene to ask that the speaker come to a conclusion.
- An object may be used as a talking stick if the group would find it helpful.

Working in pairs or small groups of 3–4

Pairs or small groups give each person time to speak in depth. These reflections need not be reported back to the whole group.

- The listener should not speak, though non-verbal signs of attention are helpful.
- It is fine for the speaker to be silent for a while if they want.
- The listener should be reminded not to respond to the first speaker when it is their turn to speak.

Group discussion

There may be times (especially in the activities of groups) when the give and take of a discussion can be appropriate – for example, when a full flow of ideas is wanted – and this might encourage some Friends to venture making contributions they were cautious of offering in other modes. It will be particularly important to encourage the quiet or reticent and not to let one or two Friends dominate the group.

In discussion, the facilitator has three main aims:

- to enable all to participate, not just the articulate and long-winded
- to keep the discussion to the point
- to prevent heated feelings from turning the discussion into an argument.

It is quite appropriate for the facilitator to ask for a minute or two of silence at any point if he or she feels this will help the group. You can also suggest that the group moves into creative listening mode so that the range of views can be heard without interruption.

Quick think

Ideas are produced rapidly (but perhaps giving someone enough time to record them) without further discussion or questioning. This is useful for bringing up a lot of suggestions that can then be used as material for a more reflective discussion.

In the following activities, text in italics indicates quotations from the lecture.

Session 1. The Kingdom is come and coming: 'realis*ing*' eschatology as the source of Quaker concern for creation

The first set of activities is designed to enable people to explore realising eschatology as the source of Quaker concern for creation.

Worship: Start your session with five minutes of opening worship.

Activity 1

['Eschatology' is] the subdiscipline of theology that explores [the] promise of hope. This hope – this assurance of a coming rightness that will rectify all that is wrong with the present – is fundamental to Christian faith.

- Ask people to reflect for a few moments for themselves on how this statement resonates with their experience and their faith. They may want to jot down some words or phrases or draw or doodle something to capture their thoughts.
- Ask people to share their reflections to this question in a pair, taking five minutes each to speak while the other person listens carefully, not replying to what is said.

Activity 2

The Kingdom of which Jesus spoke captured the imagination and sparked the hope of the people precisely because it stood in opposition to the kingdoms of this world.

- In the same pair, ask people to again take five minutes each to share their understanding of the word 'Kingdom' from their experience and in light of the lecture.

Activity 3

"[Early Friends] were simply connecting [the] cosmic outward activity of Christ with the spiritual rebirth within believers … providing individuals with a thrilling sense of participation in history and communion with the divine, grafting them into the body of God" (Dandelion and Martin, 2015: 130). To live in the Kingdom is to be united with the power and love of God, and to participate in God's work of transformation in the world, right here, right now.

- Staying in the pairs from activities 1 and 2, join with another pair to form a group of four.
- Ask people to take one minute each to share key points from their responses to both the previous questions.
- Ask people to share their understanding and experience of "participating in God's work of transformation" in the context of the more common Quaker concepts of 'faith and action' and 'faith in action'.

Activity 4
Come back together as a whole group and ask people to share one thing that has struck them or resonated with them from the session.

Worship: Close your session with five minutes of worship.

Session 2. Staying low: Jay O'Hara and the prophetic ministry of our time

Worship: Start your session with five minutes of opening worship.

Activity 1

- Ask people to share which aspect or aspects of Jay's story most resonated with them. Depending on the size of the group, you can do this in pairs, in threes or as a whole group.

Activity 2

- Ask people to share whether they have experienced the difference between "pushing the boulder up the proverbial hill" and "starting the snowball rolling down"? What did each of these feel like? Depending on the size of the group, you can do this in pairs, in threes or as a whole group.

Activity 3

- Ask people to reflect for a few moments for themselves on whether they have been in a situation where, like Jay, they felt they had to stop doing something because although it *seemed* like the right thing to do, it didn't *feel* like the right thing to do. How did they deal with the consequences of this?
- Ask people to share their reflections on this question in pairs, taking five minutes each to speak while the other person listens carefully, not replying to what is said.

Activity 4

- Working in small groups (threes or fours), ask people to reflect on and discuss what they think the role of a meeting is in drawing out and holding accountable the prophetic ministry of its members. Do you have experience of this being done well, or not so well?
- In the same groups, think about how a meeting can help individuals to rightly distinguish between the voice of God and the many other voices impinging on their attention. What are the challenges for meetings and individuals in doing this?

Activity 5: worship sharing

- Come back together as a whole group and ask people to share one thing that has struck them or resonated with them from the session.

Worship: Close your session with five minutes of worship.

Session 3. Beginning, end and new beginning: consideration of selected biblical texts

Worship: Start your session with five minutes of opening worship.

Activity 1
- Ask people to share how they read the Bible personally, and what meaning(s) it has for them. Depending on the size of the group, you can do this in pairs, in threes or as a whole group.
- As a group, reflect on how you read the Bible in your meeting.

Activity 2
The book addresses two sections of the Bible (most of this was not included in the spoken lecture so you will have to work from the book rather than the video for this activity). The questions below look at these in turn. Ask people to share their responses to these questions in a pair or small group.
- In relation to the section on Genesis 1:26–31, what is your reaction to the analysis of the words 'subdue' and 'dominion'?
- The text looks at the concept of stewardship. Does its approach to this term chime with your experience? What does it say in relation to the responsibility humans have regarding climate breakdown?
- The lecture includes an interpretation of the second passage addressed in chapter 3 (Romans 8:19–23) through the lens of childbirth. Does this lens offer you a new and different understanding? How is that helpful to you?

Activity 3
- Come back together as a whole group and ask people to share one thing that has struck them or resonated with them from the session.

Worship: Close your session with five minutes of worship.

Session 4. A green oasis: gardening as resistance in occupied Palestine

Worship: Start your session with 10 minutes of opening worship.

Activity 1

- Ask people to reflect for a few moments for themselves on their experience of living in a built-up environment and the importance to them of green spaces. They may want to jot down some words or phrases or draw or doodle something to capture their thoughts.
- Ask people to share their reflections on this question in pairs.
- Ask the pairs to reflect on how the experience of the Friends School in Ramallah resonates with their experience.

Activity 2

- Staying in the pairs from activity 1, ask the pairs to join with another pair to form groups of four.
- Ask people to take one minute each to share key points from their responses to the previous questions.
- In this part of the lecture, gardening is put forward as a symbol of hope. How does this resonate with your experience?
- As a group, think of three actions that you (as individuals, groups or a meeting) do to make hope tangible in your life.
- Ask each group to feed back to the whole group.

Activity 3

- Ask people to work in small groups. Ask each group to identify any key needs in the local community – what are the financial, emotional, physical, and spiritual needs of your neighbours, in so far as you know them? How far are those with these needs being given hope?
- Are there ways in which your meeting could bring hope to others through the use of green spaces? If your meeting doesn't have a green space of its own, are there groups you could work with to make use of green spaces in your community?

Activity 4

- Come back together as a whole group and ask people to share one thing that has struck them or resonated with them from the session.

Worship: Close your session with five minutes of worship.

Session 5. Unity with the creation: themes from Quaker experience

Worship: Start your session with 10 minutes of opening worship.

Activity 1
- Start in threes and ask each person to take five minutes each to share a time when being in or close to nature was a spiritual experience for them.
- After each person has shared, ask them to spend a further five minutes each identifying how this relates to their understanding and experience of Quakerism.
- How does this affect your engagement with the natural world and your approach to environmental activism?

Activity 2
George Fox describes his transformational spiritual encounter with the Living Christ [by declaring] that "all the creation gave another smell unto me than before, beyond what words can utter" (Fox, 1952: 27). This heightened awareness of nature became a characteristic feature of Quaker spirituality – to be united with God was also to be brought into unity with the creation.
- Staying in the threes from activity 1, ask people to join with another three to form groups of six. Consider the following questions:
  - Is this idea of unity with the creation still a characteristic feature of Quaker spirituality in your experience?
  - How does this idea affect your day-to-day choices about how you live, how you travel and what you eat?

Activity 3
The lecture records the response of British Friends to the ministry of John Woolman as being: "If he has this faith to himself, they can be easy with him; but desire to be excused if he is proposed as an example."[2]

---

2   As relayed in Sheppard (1879: 254).

- Staying in the groups from activity 2, consider the following questions:
  - Is our holding up of Friends like Woolman as 'Quaker saints' a way of excusing ourselves from following his example?
  - How does this example affect your response to the activists in your Quaker community?

Activity 4

- Staying in the groups from activity 3, consider the following question in light of the quotation in activity 3:
  - How might you follow the example set by Woolman in your life?

Activity 5

- Come back together as a whole group and ask people to share one thing that has struck them or resonated with them from the session.

Worship: Close your session with five minutes of worship.

Session 6. Hope as an act of will: tree planting in Kenya

Worship: Start your session with 10 minutes of opening worship.

Activity 1
In the lecture, we are offered the following reasons for planting trees (pages 96–97):
- peace
- human health
- beauty
- microclimate protection
- economic sustainability
- recovery of a holistic gospel
- recovery of indigenous knowledge
- climate change.
- Ask people to share their reasons for engaging in acts of hope in relation to climate breakdown. Depending on the size of the group, you can do this in pairs, in threes or as a whole group.

Activity 2
- Working in groups of three or four, ask people to consider the following questions:
  - Are you aware of the risks of tree cutting in your area?
  - Do you engage with those pursuing tree cutting to try to understand the reasons and stand in the way of tree cutting that is not absolutely essential?

Activity 3
- Working in groups of three or four, ask people to consider the following questions:
  - What is the balance between campaigning for systemic change and undertaking personal action? How can we find that balance?
  - What would be the equivalent action in your community to tree planting in Kenya?
- Ask each group to feed back to the whole group.

Activity 4

- As a meeting, consider how you might undertake one or more of the actions identified in activity 3. What would be required to make this possible? Who might you work with, and what opportunities for action are there?

Activity 5

- Come back together as a whole group and ask people to share one thing that has struck them or resonated with them from the session.

Worship: Close your session with five minutes of worship.

Session 7. Fierce hope: the spiritual condition that gives rise to transformation

Worship: Start your session with 10 minutes of opening worship.

Activity 1

- Look at Yale University's six unique audiences on how different people respond to global warming (pages 103–104 and Yale Program on Climate Change Communication, 2019).
- Ask people to think of someone they know who is in each of the six types identified (Alarmed, Concerned, Cautious, Disengaged, Doubtful, and Dismissive). This could be a family member, friend, colleague, etc.
- Once you have identified someone for each group (each person does not need to identify six, as long as the group as a whole identifies someone for each of the six groups):
  - Divide the group into six and allocate one of the six audiences to each group.
  - As a group, think about how you would effectively speak to the person in that group and encourage them to make changes in their lives.
  - Ask each group to feed back to the whole group.

Activity 2

- Working in groups of three or four, ask people to share their experience (by way of examples) of how they cope with the fear that comes with growing awareness of climate breakdown. What gives them hope?

Activity 3

In the lecture, Eden gives the example of Welling Hall, a Quaker, political scientist and artist who "is called to a ministry of making what she calls 'political art'. She works in various media in order to give shape and expression to the horror of violence, finding, as she does so, that 'the best antidote to horror is intense aesthetic engagement' (Ashley and Hall, 2018)."

- In the same groups as activity 2, ask people to share how this resonates with them. Have they experienced instances when imagination and creativity helped them to move from fear to hope?

Activity 4

Eden writes that "it is out of being broken that we can become useful to God. For, as we are reminded in Psalm 51, 'the sacrifice acceptable to God is a broken spirit; a broken and contrite heart, O God, you will not despise.'" This passage speaks to grief rather than fear. It allows us to see a way past and through our own complicity in the climate breakdown we face.

- Ask people to reflect for a few moments on their response to these ideas. They may want to jot down some words or phrases or draw or doodle to capture their thoughts.
- Ask people to share their reflections to this question in pairs, taking five minutes each to speak while the other person listens carefully.
- Ask each pair to join with another pair and consider whether there are ways in which you or your meeting could engage with this model of grief for what has been lost in any way. What might you do in response?
- Ask each group to feed back to the whole group.

Activity 5

- Come back together as a whole group and ask people to share one thing that has struck them or resonated with them from the session.

Worship: Close your session with five minutes of worship.

GLOSSARY OF THEOLOGICAL TERMS

Some of the theological terms in this lecture may be unfamiliar to Friends. I have tried, as much as possible, to define words as I used them, but this compilation of terms might prove useful as a reference.

Anthropocentric: placing humanity at the centre of consideration, or regarding humanity to be of greatest importance.

Anthropology: in theological terminology, this is the study of the nature and purpose of humanity.

Anthropomorphise: to metaphorically describe non-human things using human attributes.

Apocalypse: literally translated as 'revelation', this is a literary genre that depicts a vision of the end times as revealed by an angel or other heavenly messenger. Apocalyptic literature in the Bible includes Isaiah 24–27 and 33, Daniel, Matthew 24, Mark 13, and Revelation.

Apostasy: turning away from true faith and embracing false teaching or practice. Early Quakers, like other radical Christians of their time, believed that the early church ceased to be the church of Jesus Christ when it became the official state religion of the Roman Empire in the 4th century, and that state churches have continued in this condition of apostasy until the present time.

Christology: the study of the nature of Jesus Christ.

Covenant: a legal contract between God and the community. The most significant covenants in the Hebrew Bible are the covenants with Adam and Eve (Genesis 1:28–30), with Noah (Genesis 9:8–17), with Abraham (Genesis 12 and 15), regarding circumcision (Genesis 17), with Moses (Exodus 19–24), and with David (2 Samuel 7). Jeremiah 31:31–34 promises a new type of covenant that will be written "on their hearts". This expectation of an eschatological epistemology is of central importance to Quaker theology.

Deism: the belief that a Creator God exists but has had no interaction with creation since its beginning.

Dispensationalism: a metanarrative of biblical history that divides God's plan into distinct periods of time, each with their own law and ethic.

Doxology: prayer that is primarily focused on praising God.

Ecclesiology: the study of the nature, purpose and right ordering of the church as a human institution and as a community of believers.

Epistemology: the philosophical study of the nature, sources and criteria of knowledge – i.e. how do we know what we know?

Eschatology: the study of the ultimate destiny and purpose of the creation.

Eucharist: the ritualised eating of bread and wine as the body and blood of Christ.

Evangelism: the proclamation of the gospel of Jesus Christ for the purpose of inviting others into an experience of faith. Evangelism is distinguished from proselytism, which is marked by coercion and exploitation.

Exegesis: the interpretation of biblical texts using the tools of critical analysis.

Gnosticism: an esoteric belief system that was declared heretical by the early church. Features of Gnosticism include belief that the world was created by the Demiurge (a lesser deity) rather than by God and is not 'good', but rather something negative to be escaped; belief in a complete separation between God and the world (and between spirit and matter); and belief in a secret knowledge accessible only to the elect.

Hermeneutics: the study of the methods of reading and interpreting sacred texts.

Millennialism/Premillennialism/Postmillennialism/Amillennialism: Millennialism is the belief in a thousand-year reign of Christ on earth, based on a literal reading of Revelation 20:1–6. Premillennialism is the belief that the Second Coming of Christ will occur before the thousand-year reign of Jesus on earth, and that his coming will be accompanied by a cataclysmic tribulation. Postmillennialism expects Jesus to come again after a thousand-year period of peace and justice on earth. Amillennialism claims that the symbolic language of a thousand-year reign is meant to signify the era of the church.

Missiology: the study of the mission of the church.

Pneumatology: the study of the nature of the Holy Spirit.

Prophesy: to receive and convey a message from God to the community for the purpose of edification, exhortation or comfort. This is one of the gifts of the Spirit listed in Romans 12:4–8.

Soteriology: the study of how it is that we are 'saved'.

Spirituality: religious experience itself, as distinct from other forms of thinking about God.

Teleology: the study of the purpose of things.

Theocracy: the form of government that positions God as the ruler, with those under God's authority receiving immediate divine guidance for the ordering of society.

Theodicy: the question of why a good God permits the manifestation of evil.

Theology: the study of the nature of God.

Theopoetics: the use of poetic and aesthetic expression, rather than rational logic, to communicate about God and spiritual experience.

Theosis: the soteriology of the Eastern Orthodox tradition, which emphasises union with God as the goal of human experience.

Trinity: the Christian doctrine that God exists as three persons (Creator, Christ and Holy Spirit) in one nature. The exact formulation in Greek of this paradoxical mystery, and the subtle nuances of its translation into other languages, was one of the most controversial issues of the first thousand years of Christianity. Early Friends rejected the speculative and philosophical nature of Trinitarian doctrine but very much affirmed the truths that doctrine was created to protect.

BIBLIOGRAPHY

Abbott, M. (2018). *Walk humbly, serve boldly: Modern Quakers as everyday prophets*. San Francisco, CA: Inner Light Books.

Adams, A. (2012). *Is there not a new creation?* Luston: Applegarth.

AjyaL Radio Network (2019). 'Friends School students participate in the tree planting event of its founding' [TV programme in Arabic], www.facebook.com/AJYAL.FM/videos/394044504784294/Uzpf STEwNzE2MDgxMjYzNzYxMToyMTkzNTI1NjQ0MDAxMTA 3:www.arn.ps, accessed 14 July 2019.

Alliance for Water Justice in Palestine (2016). 'Facts #136 and index', www.waterjusticeinpalestine.org/weeklyfacts, accessed 18 July 2019.

Ambler, R. (1990). 'Befriending the earth: A theological challenge' in *Friends Quarterly*, 26(1), 7–17.

Amnesty International (2009). *Troubled waters: Palestinians denied fair access to water*. London: Amnesty International.

Ashley, C., and W. Hall. (2018). 'A Friend in Washington explores art, faith, and advocacy at FCNL', Friends Committee on National Legislation,www.fcnl.org/updates/a-friend-in-washington-explores-art-faith-and-advocacy-at-fcnl-1667, accessed 18 July 2019.

Ashworth, T. (2006). *Paul's necessary sin: The experience of liberation*. Farnham: Ashgate.

Barker, D., and D. Bearce (2012). 'End-times theology, the shadow of the future, and public resistance to addressing global climate change' in *Political Research Quarterly*, 66(2), 267–279.

Beals, C. (2013). 'Dividing and conquering: The dualistic roots of environmentalism and its foes' in *Quaker Religious Thought*, 121, 5–13.

Benezet, A. (1778). *A first book for children*. Philadelphia: J. Crukshank.

Bock, C. (2016). 'Climatologists, theologians, and prophets: Toward an ecotheology of critical hope' in *CrossCurrents*, 66(1), 8–34.

Bock, C. (2018). 'Quakers and the Eco-Reformation', presentation at Quaker Heritage Day 2018, Berkeley Friends Church, Berkeley, CA, 10 March, www.berkeleyfriendschurch.org/qhd/recent-quaker-heritage-day-speakers/qhd-2018-with-cherice-bock-quakers-and-the-eco-reformation, accessed 17 July 2019.

Boulding, K. (1966). 'The economics of the coming spaceship earth' in H. Jarrett, ed., *Environmental quality in a growing economy*. Baltimore: Johns Hopkins University Press, pp. 3–14.

Brueggemann, W. (2001). *The prophetic imagination*. 2nd ed. Minneapolis: Augsburg Fortress.

Brunner, D., J. Butler and A. Swoboda (2014). *Introducing evangelical ecotheology: Foundations in scripture, theology, history, and praxis*. Grand Rapids, MI: Baker Academic.

Bruyneel, S. (2015). 'Margaret Fell and the Second Coming of Christ' in S. Angell and P. B. Dandelion, eds., *Early Quakers and their theological thought 1647–1723*. New York: Cambridge University Press, pp. 102–117.

Burrough, E. (1672). *The memorable works of a son of thunder and consolation*. London: E. Hookes/Society of Friends.

Calvin, J. (1948). *Commentaries on the first book of Moses called Genesis*, volume 1. Translated by John King. Grand Rapids, MI: W. B. Eerdmans, p. 96.

Climate Disobedience Center (2017). 'Jay O'Hara', www.climatedisobedience.org/jayohara, accessed 18 July 2019.

Collins, P. (2011). 'The development of ecospirituality among British Quakers' in *European Journal of Literature, Culture and Environment*, 2(2), 83–99.

Connell, J. (2014). 'Let the holy seed of life reign: Perfection, Pelagianism, and the early Friends' in *Quaker Theology*, 24, http://quakertheology.org/Connell-Are-Quakers-Pelagians.html, accessed 17 July 2019.

Cooper, W. (1960). 'Quaker perspectives of the nature of man' in *Quaker Religious Thought*, 4, 2–20.

Dandelion, B. P. (1996). *A sociological analysis of the theology of Quakers: The silent revolution*. Lewiston, NY: Edwin Mellen Press.

Dandelion, B. P., D. Gwyn and T. Peat (2018). *Heaven on earth: Quakers and the Second Coming*. 2nd ed. Philadelphia and Birmingham: Plain Press.

Dandelion, B. P., and F. Martin (2015). '"Outcasts of Israel": The apocalyptic theology of Edward Burrough and Francis Howgill' in S. Angell and B. P. Dandelion, eds., *Early Quakers and their theological thought 1647–1723*. New York: Cambridge University Press, pp. 118–136.

Drayton, B. (2012). *Climate change: A spiritual challenge & Becoming again a witnessing body: Two letters to New England Friends from Brian Drayton*. Boston: Beacon Hill Friends House.

Drayton, B., and W. P. Taber, Jr. (2016). *A language for the inward landscape: Spiritual wisdom from the Quaker movement*. Philadelphia: Tract Association of Friends.

Drollinger, R. (2018). *Coming to grips with the religion of environmentalism*, Capitol Ministries, http://capmin.org/coming-to-grips-with-the-religion-of-environmentalism, accessed 18 July 2019.

Eco, U. (1984) *Semiotics and the philosophy of language*. Bloomington: Indiana University Press.

Emmerich, R., dir. (2004). *The day after tomorrow* [film], Centropolis Entertainment, Lions Gate Films and Mark Gordon Company.

Encyclical letter Laudato si' of the Holy Father Francis on care for our common home (2015). Vatican City: Vatican Press.

Famine Early Warning Systems Network (2019). 'Food security outlook update: April 2019', www.fews.net/east-africa/kenya/food-security-outlook-update/april-2019, accessed 6 May 2019.

Feinberg, M., and R. Willer (2011). 'Apocalypse soon? Dire messages reduce belief in global warming by contradicting just-world beliefs' in *Psychological Science*, 22(1), 34–38.

Fox, G. (1831). *The works of George Fox*, volume 7. Philadelphia: Marcus T. C. Gould.

Fox, G. (1952). *The journal of George Fox*, ed. J. L. Nickalls. Cambridge: Cambridge University Press.

Freiday, D. (1990). 'Response [to V. Schurman]' in *Quaker Religious Thought*, 74, 43–48.

Friends World Committee for Consultation (2006). 'Kinds of Friends', http://fwcc.world/kinds-of-friends, accessed 18 July 2019.

Gajanan, M. (2017). 'Republican Congressman says God will "take care of" climate change' in *Time*, 31 May, www.time.com/4800000/tim-walberg-god-climate-change, accessed 18 July 2019.

Gasteyer, S., J. Isaac, J. Hillal and S. Walsh (2012). 'Water grabbing in colonial perspective: Land and water in Israel/Palestine' in *Water Alternatives*, 5(2), 450–468.

George Fox University (2019). 'Creation care specialization', www. georgefox.edu/seminary/programs/specializations/creation-care. html, accessed 18 July 2019.

Granberg-Michaelson, W. (2018). 'Crimes against creation' in *Sojourners*, www.sojo.net/articles/crimes-against-creation, accessed 12 April 2019.

Guiton, G. (2009). 'Recovering the lost radiance: The kingdom of God, the early Friends, and the future of Quakerism' in *Quaker Religious Thought*, 113, 28–50.

Guiton, G. (2012). *The early Quakers and the 'Kingdom of God'*. San Francisco: Inner Light Books.

Guiton, G. (2019). *Where heaven and earth are one: Following 'the way', caring for the planet*, www.gerardguiton.com/wp-content/ uploads/2019/05/Where-Heaven-and-Earth-are-One.docx, accessed 18 May 2019.

Gummere, A. M. (1922). *The journal and essays of John Woolman*. New York: Macmillan, p. 327.

Gwyn, D. (2014). *A sustainable life: Quaker faith and practice in the renewal of creation*. Philadelphia: QuakerPress of Friends General Conference.

Gwyn, D. (2015). 'Seventeenth-century context and Quaker beginnings' in S. Angell and P. B. Dandelion, eds., *Early Quakers and their theological thought 1647–1723*. New York: Cambridge University Press, pp. 13–31.

Gwyn, D. (2018). 'Come again?' in B. P. Dandelion, D. Gwyn and T. Peat, *Heaven on earth: Quakers and the Second Coming*. 2nd ed. Philadelphia and Birmingham: Plain Press, pp. 93–109.

Haidt, J. (2013). *The righteous mind: Why good people are divided by politics and religion*. New York: Vintage Books.

Head, T. (1981). 'Everyday eschatology: The witness of Quaker simplicity' in D. Freiday, ed., *The day of the Lord: Eschatology in Quaker perspective*. Newberg, OR: Barclay Press, pp. 11–21.

Heidorn, K. C. (1999). 'Luke Howard: The man who named the clouds' in *The Weather Doctor*, www.islandnet.com/~see/weather/ history/howard.htm, accessed 18 July 2019.

Hiebert, T. (1996). 'Rethinking dominion theology' in *Direction: A Mennonite Brethren Forum*, 25(2), 16–25.

Hinshaw, C. (1964). *Apology for perfection*. Wallingford: Pendle Hill.

Hodson, M., and M. Hodson (2017). *An introduction to environmental ethics*. Cambridge: Grove Books.

Howgill, M. (1662). *The vision of the Lord of Hosts*, www.woodbrooke. org.uk/wp-content/uploads/2017/02/QHC80_Howgill_M.txt, accessed 18 July 2019.

Howgill, F. (1672). 'A testimony' in E. Burrough, *The memorable works of a son of thunder and consolation*. London: E. Hookes/Society of Friends.

Jones, J. (2012). 'A theological interpretation of "Viriditas" in Hildegard of Bingen and Gregory the Great', Bu.edu, www. bu.edu/pdme/jeannette-jones, accessed 11 April 2019.

Kassühlke, R. (1974). 'An attempt at a dynamic equivalent translation of Basileia Tou Theou' in *The Bible Translator*, 25(2), 236–238.

Keefe-Perry, K., and C. Keefe-Perry (2018). 'Jay O'Hara' [podcast], On Carrying a Concern, www.ocacshow.org/episodes/2018/4/13/episode-04-jay-ohara, accessed 14 May 2019.

Kelley, D. (1982). '"A tender regard to the whole creation": Anthony Benezet and the emergence of an eighteenth-century Quaker ecology' in *Pennsylvania Magazine of History and Biography*, 106, 69–88.

Kelley, D. (1985). 'The evolution of Quaker theology and the unfolding of a distinctive Quaker ecological perspective in eighteenth-century America' in *Pennsylvania History: A Journal of Mid-Atlantic Studies*, 52(4), 242–253.

Kelly, T. (1996). *A testament of devotion*. New York: HarperCollins Publishers.

Klein, N. (2014). *This changes everything: Capitalism vs the climate*. New York: Simon & Schuster.

Lunn, P. (2011). *Costing not less than everything: Sustainability and spirituality in challenging times*. London: Quaker Books.

Luther, M. (1955). *Luther's works*, ed. J. Pelikan. St Louis: Concordia Publishing House.

Maathai, W. (2004). 'Nobel lecture', Oslo, 10 December, www. nobelprize.org/prizes/peace/2004/maathai/26050-wangari-maathai-nobel-lecture-2004, accessed 17 July 2019.

Martin, F. (2012). *Reinterpreting early Quaker eschatology for Friends today*. Unpublished paper, Andover-Newton Theological School.

Matere, J., P. Simpkin, J. Angerer, et al. (2019). 'Predictive Livestock Early Warning System (PLEWS): Monitoring forage condition and implications for animal production in Kenya' in *Weather and Climate Extremes*, www.doi.org/10.1016/j.wace.2019.100209, accessed 6 May 2019.

McFague, S. (1998). 'The world as God's body' in *The Christian Century*, 20–27 July, 671–673.

Meyer, N., dir. (1983). *The day after* [film], ABC Circle Films.

Michaelis, L. (2017). *Gleanings*. London: Friend Publications.

Michaelson, J. (2015). 'Pope Francis' environmental encyclical is even more radical than it appears' in *Sojourners*, www.sojo.net/articles/pope-francis-environmental-encyclical-even-more-radical-it-appears, accessed 12 April 2019.

Middleton, W. (1925). 'John Bartram, botanist' in *Scientific Monthly*, 21(2), 191–216.

Miller, T. (2013). 'Kingdoms in conflict: Examining the use of "Kingdom of Heaven" in Matthew', Maranatha Baptist Seminary, www.mbu.edu/seminary/kingdoms-in-conflict-examining-the-use-of-kingdom-of-heaven-in-matthew, accessed 5 May 2019.

Morries, G. (2009). *From revelation to resource: The natural world in the thought and experience of Quakers in Britain and Ireland 1647–1830* [PhD thesis], University of Birmingham.

Mother Teresa (2003). *Come be my light* (official commemorative edition). n.p.: Missionaries of Charity.

MSNBC (2015). 'Prosecutor and activist align for the environment' [video], www.youtube.com/watch?v=iEYPXUtBwnA, accessed 15 July 2019.

Muers, R. (2015). *Testimony: Quakerism and theological ethics*. London: SCM Press.

Nam, R. (2013). 'Intertextuality and the relationship of humankind among fish, birds, and creeping things' in *Quaker Religious Thought*, 121, 22–30.

National Association of Evangelicals (2011). *Loving the least of these: Addressing a changing environment*. Washington, DC: National Association of Evangelicals.

New World Encyclopedia Editors (2019). 'Oslo Accords' in *New World Encyclopedia*, www.newworldencyclopedia.org/entry/Oslo_Accords, accessed 18 July 2019.

Nobel Committee (2004). 'The Nobel Peace Prize for 2004' [press release], www.nobelprize.org/prizes/peace/2004/press-release, accessed 18 July 2019.

Nuttall, G. (1947). '"Unity with the creation": George Fox and the hermetic philosophy' in *Friends Quarterly*, 1, 134–143.

O'Hara, J. (2015). 'Climate change: An invitation to new life?' [video], TEDxNewBedford, www.youtube.com/watch?v=GPLbjoDDrdo, accessed 15 April 2019.

O'Hara, J. (2018). 'Finding the Quaker core: Are we ready to be relevant in the 21st century?', 2018 Ernest and Esther Weed Memorial Lecture, Beacon Hill Friends House, Boston, 29 April.

Penington, I. (1679). Letter dated 4 March 1679 in *Works of Isaac Penington*, Quaker Heritage Press, www.qhpress.org/texts/penington/letter96.html, accessed 18 July 2019.

Perrin, N. (1974). 'Eschatology and hermeneutics: Reflections on method in the interpretation of the New Testament' in *Journal of Biblical Literature*, 93(1), 3–14.

Plank, G. (2007). '"The flame of life was kindled in all animal and sensitive creatures": One Quaker colonist's view of animal life' in *Church History*, 76(3), 569–590.

Pyle, M. (2013). 'Out of darkness into light' in *Friends Journal*, 1 November, www.friendsjournal.org/darkness-light, accessed 18 July 2019.

QuakerSpeak (2015). 'Why I blockaded 40,000 tons of coal with a lobster boat' [video], www.quakerspeak.com/why-i-blockaded-40000-tons-of-coal-with-a-lobster-boat, accessed 15 April 2019.

Rasmussen, L. (1995). 'The integrity of creation: What can it mean for Christian ethics?' in *Annual of the Society of Christian Ethics*, 15, 161–175.

Reser, J., and G. Bradley (2017). 'Fear appeals in climate change communication' in *Oxford Research Encyclopedias: Climate Science*, https://oxfordre.com/climatescience/view/ 10.1093/acrefore/9780190228620.001.0001/acrefore-9780190228620-e-386, accessed 17 July 2019.

Ross, E. (2012). 'The solace of history: Reflections on Quakers and the environment' in *Friends Journal*, 58, 15–18.

Santmire, H. (1985). *The travail of nature: The ambiguous ecological promise of Christian theology*. Minneapolis: Fortress Press.

Schilling, J., M. Akuno, J. Scheffran, and T. Weinzierl (2014). 'On raids and relations: Climate change and pastoral conflict in Northern Kenya' in S. Bronkhorst and U. Bob, eds., *Conflict-sensitive adaptation to climate change in Africa*. Berlin: Berliner Wissenschafts-Verlag, pp. 241–268.

Schurman, V. (1990). 'A Quaker theology of the stewardship of creation' in *Quaker Religious Thought*, 74, 27–41.

Scott, B. (1989). *Hear then the parable: A commentary on the parables of Jesus*. Minneapolis: Fortress Press, pp. 56–62.

Sheppard, M. (1879). *Selections from the letters and memoranda of Mary M. Sheppard*. n.p.: William H. Pile.

Skrimshire, S. (2014). 'Climate change and apocalyptic faith' in *Wiley Interdisciplinary Reviews: Climate Change*, 5, 233–246.

Snyman, G. (2011). 'Empire and a hermeneutics of vulnerability' in *Studia Historiae Ecclesiasticae*, 37, 1–20.

Snyman, G. (2015). 'Responding to the decolonial turn: Epistemic vulnerability' in *Missionalia: Southern African Journal of Mission Studies*, 43(3), 266–291.

Sox, D. (2009). 'Quakers and the natural order' in *Journal of the Friends Historical Society*, 61(3), 175–186.

Spencer, C. (2004). 'Holiness: The Quaker way of perfection' in *Quaker History*, 93(1), 123–147.

Swennerfelt, R. (2016). *Rising to the challenge: The transition movement and people of faith*. Caye Caulker: Producciones de la Hamaca.

Taber, W. (1980). 'The theology of the inward imperative: Traveling Quaker ministry of the middle period' in *Quaker Religious Thought*, 50, 3–19.

TheLoizeauxGroupLLC (2019). 'Brayton Point power plant cooling towers: Controlled Demolition, Inc.' [video], www.youtube.com/watch?v=fbw1lhpduGw, accessed 18 July 2019.

Thomas, A. (1995). *Only fellow-voyagers: Creation stories as guides for the journey*. London: Quaker Home Service and Woodbrooke College for the Swarthmore Lecture Committee.

Tippett, K. (2011). 'Walter Brueggemann: The prophetic imagination' [radio show], *On Being*, 22 December, https://onbeing.org/programs/walter-brueggemann-the-prophetic-imagination-dec2018, accessed 18 July 2019.

Treadway, C., N. Bowles, C. Ansell, et al. (2008). 'Caring for creation' [whole issue] in *Journal of the North Carolina Yearly Meeting (Conservative)*, 5.

United Nations Environment Programme (2003). *Desk study on the environment in the Occupied Palestinian Territories*. Geneva: United Nations Environment Programme.

van der Linden, S., E. Maibach and A. Leiserowitz (2015). 'Improving public engagement with climate change: Five "best practice" insights from psychological science' in *Perspectives on Psychological Science*, 10(6), 758–763.

Veldman, R. (2013). 'Does end time belief really cause climate change apathy?' in *Religion Dispatches*, www.religiondispatches.org/does-end-time-belief-really-cause-climate-change-apathy, accessed 12 April 2019.

Vox, L. (2017). 'Why don't Christian conservatives worry about climate change? God' in *Washington Post*, www.washingtonpost.com/posteverything/wp/2017/06/02/why-dont-christian-conservatives-worry-about-climate-change-god/?utm_term=.4923c3c97b06, accessed 17 July 2019.

Ward, K. and J. O'Hara (2014). 'Invitation to attend the trial', *LobsterBoatBlockade*, https://lobsterboatblockade.org/the-trial/invitation, accessed 18 July 2019.

Watson, E. (1982). *Daughters of Zion*. Richmond, IN: Friends United Press.

Watson, E. (1990). *The cool green hills of earth*. Philadelphia: Wider Quaker Fellowship.

Watson, E. (1991). *Healing ourselves and the earth*. 2nd ed. Burlington: Quaker Earthcare Witness.

Watson, E. (1997). *Wisdom's daughters*. Eugene, OR: Wipf and Stock.

White, L., Jr (1967). 'The historical roots of our ecological crisis' in *Science*, 155, 1203–1207.

Wilcox, A. (2019). 'Quakers and the prophetic tradition', 14 April, www.ashleymwilcox.com/blog/2019/4/14/quakers-and-the-prophetic-tradition, accessed 18 July 2010.

Williams, R. (2005). 'Ecology and economy', lecture at the University of Kent, Canterbury, 8 March, http://aoc2013.brix.fatbeehive.com/articles.php/1550/ecology-and-economy-archbishop-calls-for-action-on-environment-to-head-off-social-crisis, accessed 17 July 2019.

Wilson, G. (1990). 'Restoring the image perspectives on a biblical view of creation' in *Quaker Religious Thought*, 74, 11–21.

Woolman, J. (1871). *The journal of John Woolman*. Boston: Osgood, p. 58.

World Conference of Friends (2012). *Kabarak Call for Peace and Ecojustice*, www.fwcc.world/call.pdf, accessed 18 July 2019.

Yale Program on Climate Change Communication (2019). 'Global warming's six Americas', https://climatecommunication.yale.edu/about/projects/global-warmings-six-americas, accessed 18 July 2019.

Zarembka, D. (2019). 'The best summary of Kenya renewable energy (& dirty energy) you can find' in *Clean Technica*, 30 March, https://cleantechnica.com/2019/03/30/the-best-summary-of-kenya-renewable-energy-dirty-energy-you-can-find, accessed 18 July 2019.